FIRST
CORINTHIANS

FIRST CORINTHIANS

by
ROBERT B. HUGHES

MOODY PRESS
CHICAGO

All Scripture quotations, unless noted otherwise, are from the *New American Standard
Bible,* © 1960, 1962, 1963, 1968, 1971, 1972, 1973, 1975, and 1977 by the Lockman
Foundation, and are used by permission.

Library of Congress Cataloging in Publication Data:

Hughes, Robert B., 1946-
  First Corinthians.

  Bibliography: p.
  1. Bible.   N.T.   Corinthians, 1st—Commentaries.
BS2675.3.H82   1985   227'.307   85-8913
ISBN: 0-8024-0447-2 (pbk.)

1 2 3 4 5 6 7 Printing/EP/90 89 88 87 86 85

Printed in the United States of America

CONTENTS

CHAPTER   PAGE

1. A Window on Corinth   7

2. Wisdom and the Cross (1:1—2:16)   21

3. Wisdom and Leadership (3:1—4:21)   46

4. Sexual and Social Purity (5:1—6:20)   61

5. Sex and Marriage: Staying or Changing (7:1-40)   74

6. Concerning Idols and Their Sacrifices (8:1—11:1)   85

7. The Traditions: Kept and Unkept (11:2-34)   109

8. The Source and Worth of Spiritual Gifts (12:1-31)   116

9. The Practice of Spiritual Gifts (13:1—14:40)   124

10. The Question of the Resurrection (15:1-58)   138

11. With a View to Paul's Future Arrival (16:1-24)   151

Selected Bibliography   155

to
Jonathan Robert Hughes,
a loving son and a generous brother

1

A WINDOW ON CORINTH

INTRODUCTION

First Corinthians speaks to people in all times and all places. But when Paul first wrote that letter, he had some specific problems to solve with a particular group of people. Instead of applying the truth in general, Paul tailored it to meet the Corinthians' specific needs. He knew what truth was needed and how to apply it. Therefore, 1 Corinthians was the result of Paul's applying what he knew about the ways of God to the particular problems and needs of the Corinthians.

The following material surveys the key problems and truths in 1 Corinthians. Several of those are illustrated by opposites—wise/foolish, strong/weak, and spiritual/unspiritual.

WISDOM AND FOOLISHNESS

Paul mentioned wisdom and foolishness over thirty times in 1 Corinthians.[1] "Wisdom" and "wise" are used twenty-three times in chapters 1-3 and occur only three more times in the remaining thirteen chapters. The topic of foolishness occurs nine times in the first three chapters. In the next thirteen chapters, the concept occurs only with reference to the apostles' being fools for Christ's sake (4:10), and to the fool who mockingly asked about the kind of body the dead would receive at the resurrection (15:36). The first chapters of the letter, therefore, focus on the contrast of wisdom and foolishness.

---

1. See " 'Wisdom' and 'Knowledge' in 1 Corinthians," in E. Earle Ellis, *Prophecy and Hermeneutics in Early Christianity* (Grand Rapids: Eerdmans, 1978), pp. 45-62.

But the Corinthians previously had their own ideas about what made a person wise or foolish. They split into factions that exalted the personalities of ministers (1:10-12); they contemplated changing their marital or social status to become more "spiritual" (7:17-24); they despised Christians who did not eat certain foods (8:9-13); they turned the Lord's table into a banquet free-for-all (11:20-22); they denied honor to the less "flashy" gifts of the Spirit (12:20-26); and they toyed with rejecting the teaching that a physical resurrection was essential for eternal life (15:12).

Paul knew those actions violated God's definitions of wisdom. He viewed the Corinthians' self-made wisdom through the cross of Christ, and he saw that their wisdom was void in its meaning and power (1:17). Presenting the solution to the problem of nullifying the cross occupied Paul throughout his letter.

KNOWLEDGE

The concepts of knowing and knowledge occur over thirty times in 1 Corinthians and are closely linked to the idea of wisdom. The Corinthians were gifted by God in the area of knowledge (1:5), but that God-given knowledge did not operate automatically. It needed to be practiced. Because the Corinthians lacked maturity, they ended up acting ignorantly in many crucial areas.

Paul, therefore, had to remind them of much they should have already known. Several of Paul's reminders started with an introductory, "Do you not know?" Did they not know that the Spirit of God dwelled in them (3:16; 6:19); that sin could infect the entire community (5:6); that Christians would judge the world (6:2); that the unrighteous would not inherit the kingdom of God (6:9); that their bodies were members of Christ (6:15); and that there was physical unity created between a man and a prostitute (6:16)?

God gave them knowledge, but that did not automatically ensure it would be practiced. The Corinthians took God's knowledge and turned it to their own selfish ends by adding other standards such as individual personality, method of ministry, and ability in speech.

By contrast, Paul reminded them of his singular but all-encompassing knowledge. He came knowing only Christ, and Him crucified (2:2). He asserted that there was only one source for true knowledge, the Spirit of God (2:11-12), and that true knowledge would always be coupled with love (8:1; 13:2). As a result, the ministering of knowledge would be intelligible, not hidden from the minds of hearers (14:11, 16).

Above all, Paul put the function and worth of knowledge into historical perspective. It was only temporary and would be done away with when the fullness of knowledge came face-to-face (13:8). Why did the Corinthians act as if their knowledge was the end of the process and eternal in scope (4:8)? It was because they did not remember their knowledge was only for the "when I was a child" (13:11) stage and would be put away like an old toy to embrace the full knowledge of God (13:8-12).

THE WEAK AND THE STRONG

One criterion for the status of wisdom in Corinth was one's social strength.[2] That included both the idea of riches and social status (1:26-28; 4:7-8; 6:5-7; 11:22). Although there was nothing inherently wrong with those things, the Corinthians began equating them with spiritual standing, to the point that they considered speaking in tongues as part of that status (12:29-31). Paul labored throughout his letter to show them where true strength and status lay, and to show that he viewed their lives through the cross of Christ (2:2).

ARROGANCE AND BOASTING

One destructive result of the Corinthians' views of wisdom and status was boasting and arrogance. The word translated "arrogant" or "puffed up" occurs six times in 1 Corinthians,

2. Gerd Theissen, "The Strong and Weak in Corinth," *The Social Setting of Pauline Christianity,* ed. John. H. Schutz (Philadelphia: Fortress, 1982), pp. 121-43.

and only once again in the New Testament in Colossians 2:18. The frequent usage of this word in 1 Corinthians sheds light on the attitudes of the Corinthian Christians.

The Corinthians were arrogant to each other (4:6). Some were arrogant in the face of Paul's upcoming visit (4:18), to which he replied that he would come and find out "not the words of those who are arrogant, but their power" (4:19). Some were arrogant about the sin of a brother (5:2). When addressing the problem of despising a weaker brother, Paul claimed that "knowledge makes arrogant, but love edifies" (8:1). In a more positive vein, Paul declared that love "is not arrogant" (13:4).

How did the Corinthians become so inflated in their self-opinion? They judged themselves and others. Once they had judged themselves (favorably, of course), they began to boast. That idea is found throughout the letter (1:29, 31; 3:21; 4:7; 5:6; 9:15-16; 15:31).

JUDGE, TEST, AND EXAMINE

Seven different Greek words for "judging" were used over thirty-five times throughout 1 Corinthians. Those words are translated "appraise," "examine," "judge," "judgment," "tempt," "try," "test," and "approved."

The Corinthians' turning to arrogance and boasting was based on faulty judgment, according to human standards. That judgment ignored the important future judgment of the Day of the Lord (4:5). Therefore, those premature judgments resulted in faulty evaluations of God's ministers (2:14-15; 4:3-4); an acceptance of sin (5:3); a secular approach to lawsuits (6:1); a fear that certain sexual and social relationships could deter Christian purity (7:1, 12-14, 17, 20, 24, 26, 36, 39); selfish evaluations of the place of meats sacrificed to idols (10:25, 27); a false evaluation of the purity of the Body of Christ at the Lord's table (11:28-29); and a tendency to misjudge the worth of spiritual gifts and prophecy (14:24).

The attitude of the Corinthians was summed up in a phrase that occurs twice in the letter: "all things are lawful" (6:12;

10:23). But they forgot the one essential addition to that statement of freedom—all things must edify.

EDIFICATION

Edification was in the opposite direction from the Corinthians' perception of freedom. Their views on wisdom, spirituality, meats, and spiritual gifts all needed the redirective force of edification (3:9; 8:1, 10; 10:23; 14:3-5, 12, 17, 26). Paul's standard for edification was the cross of Christ, the very thing the Corinthians were nullifying in their efforts to maintain status (1:17).

AUTHORITY

Though Paul's consistent solution to those problems was applying the cross of Christ, at one point he dealt with criticism of his ministry by including the concept of authority. The defense of his authority occurs in chapter nine and centers on his rights to work or not to work (9:6, 12). The Corinthians concluded that because Paul did not accept their support, he was inferior to other apostles. Paul dealt with that criticism at length in 2 Corinthians 11-12. In 1 Corinthians 9, however, he revealed his underlying reason for not accepting support and other facets of apostolic privilege: he wanted to identify with all groups in order to save as many as possible (9:19-22). The Corinthians missed the working of the cross of Christ because they focused on worldly standards of status.

WORLD

The Corinthians tended to be worldly in their thinking. In order to correct that mindset, Paul presented the true context for their wrong desires. He used two words for that concept, "age" and "world." Paul contrasted the worth of this age with: God's evaluation of it based on the cross of Christ (1:20, 27-28; 3:18-19); the insight brought by the Spirit (2:6-8); the hostile attitude of some toward the apostles (4:9-13); the final subjection of the world to judgment by the saints (6:2); and the world's temporary and condemned nature (7:31; 11:32).

THE CROSS OF CHRIST

When confronted with the Corinthians' problems, the truth that sprang to Paul's mind and controlled his thoughts and words was the truth of Christ.

Concerning the problem of division and arrogance in the community (1:18—6:20), Paul applied the cross in wisdom (1-4, especially 1:13 and 4:7). He applied the cross to immorality in the body (5-6; especially 5:7 and 6:19-20). When confronting the problem of false and true sexual purity (7:1-40), Paul applied the cross to the adequacy of their calling (7:17). For the problem of self-limitation and lack of edification (8:1—11:1), he showed how the cross demanded the kind of freedom that edified and saved (8:12; 10:15-16).

For the problem of community order (11:2—14:40), Paul applied the cross to the life of the church and its freedom to love and edify (11:27; 12:12). Facing the problem of doubt about the resurrection (15:1-58), Paul applied the cross to the new order of the resurrection (15:20-28).

Paul did not address a single problem without relating that problem to the work of God through Christ. That is not only a revelation into the mind of Paul, but also of how we should learn to address our own problems and those of the world around us.

Broad Structural Overview

The letter is framed by two mentions of Paul's itinerary. The first is in 4:18-21 and served as a transition to the weighty matters in chapters 5-15, especially chapter 5. It was a harsh and threatening statement of his intentions to come and judge. But it was also a loving plea that Paul might come in love and gentleness.

At the second mention of his pending arrival (16:3-9), he revealed that he would not be coming to Corinth by sea directly from Ephesus. Instead, he would come to them by the land route that passed through Macedonia. The Corinthian reaction to that change of itinerary is clearly seen throughout 2 Corinthians. But its effect on the contents of 1 Corinthians was to place Paul's pending arrival before the readers in the hope that they would solve their problems before he arrived.[3]

Therefore, the discussions of purity (5:1—7:40), idols and sacrifices (8:1—11:1), traditions (11:2-33), spiritual gifts (12:1—14:40), and the resurrection (15:1-58) were framed within the fact of Paul's coming either in love or in discipline.

PAUL'S PRIOR RELATIONS WITH CORINTH[4]

The problems highlighted in the section above may be summarized as follows. The Corinthians had fallen into serious errors based on arrogance developed from worldly wisdom that focused on riches, social standing, and personality traits. Paul was judged as an inferior apostle, one who could be left behind (4:6, 8) as the Corinthians marched on in their kingdom living. Paul's speech and life-style were criticized. But he was used to such criticism. A brief look at his life before Corinth will help us understand how God prepared him for addressing the Corinthians' problems.

FROM MACEDONIA TO ATHENS

Paul had thought through one area of criticism, his work and support, long before he entered Corinth. In the Thessalonian correspondence he argued that Christians ought to work for their food (1 Thess. 2:7-10), and he used himself as a model of self-support (2 Thess. 3:6-15). Paul addressed that world view at length in 1 Corinthians 9.

Paul, during much persecution, left Thessalonica, passed through Berea (Acts 17:10), and entered Athens. Paul sarcastically used his persecuted life-style to show how far he had been left behind by the exalted and reigning Corinthians (1 Cor. 4:8-14).

---

3. For a survey of the various kinds of problems faced, see E. Earle Ellis, "Paul and His Opponents," *Prophecy and Hermeneutics in Early Christianity* (Grand Rapids: Eerdmans, 1978), pp. 80-115.
4. See R. B. Hughes, *Second Corinthians* (Chicago: Moody, 1983), pp. 14-21.

Cities of Paul's Aegean Itinerary

THE FIRST VISIT TO CORINTH

Paul came to Corinth (Acts 18:1) in weakness, fear, and trembling (1 Cor. 2:1-5). He labored with Priscilla and Aquila in the making of tents (Acts 18:3), an endeavor that would be thrown back in his face as an indication that he was neither strong nor using his full apostolic rights (1 Cor. 9:6, 15; 2 Cor. 11:7-9; 12:13).

Paul endured a lot of hostility in Corinth—so much so that the Lord gave him a special vision telling him not to fear (Acts 18:9-10). When Paul was taken to court by the Jewish leaders, the verdict of Gallio the judge[5] was that Christianity was only a problem of religious differences within the Jewish faith (Acts 18:12-17). That did not stop the physical abuse, however (Acts 18:17).

Even though the Corinthians had several opportunities to observe their apostle undergoing persecution, some had determined that such a life was all right for Paul, but certainly was not for them. The Corinthians apparently had forgotten, or never realized, that Paul's suffering was not only a link to Christ's suffering, but also had implications for their own life-styles.

Paul stayed in Corinth at least one-and-one-half years (Acts 18:11), and then he returned home to Antioch in Syria.

THE SECOND VISIT TO CORINTH

The second visit of Paul to Corinth was only briefly mentioned in 2 Corinthians 13:2. But that visit was of great importance.

> I have previously said when present the second time, and though now absent I say in advance to those who have sinned in the past and to all the rest as well, that if I come again, I will not spare anyone, since you are seeking for proof of the Christ who speaks in me, and who is not weak toward you, but mighty in you. (2 Cor. 13:2-3).

Those verses highlight several important insights into the situation before, during, and after the second visit. (1) The problem was so severe during Paul's second visit that he had to threaten severe discipline. (2) That threat was made with reference to his return, because the situation was not corrected during his second visit. Paul concluded that he should depart and in absence work to solve the problem. (3) The problem centered on proof that Christ spoke through Paul (2 Cor. 13:3). Did he have acceptable credentials? Some were saying no.

5. The dates of Gallio's rule place Paul in Corinth around A.D., 50-52. See N. G. L. Hammond and H. H. Scullard, eds., *The Oxford Classical Dictionary,* 2d ed. (Oxford: Clarendon, 1970), s.v. "Gallio."

There is much debate over whether Paul's second visit was before or after the writing of 1 Corinthians.[6] The itinerary followed in this commentary concludes that Paul heard about the problems in Corinth when he arrived in Ephesus on his second missionary journey (Acts 19:1-20). He made the second visit to Corinth (not recorded in Acts), where he did what he could to gain a hearing. That attempt failed, and Paul left with an ultimatum: if he returned he would spare no one (2 Cor. 13:2). Then, after his departure, he sent a letter telling the Corinthians to avoid immoral Christians (1 Cor. 5:9), no doubt speaking to the primary issue of debate during his second visit. Later, Paul wrote 1 Corinthians to clear up both new and old problems. Second Corinthians was written shortly afterward.[7]

That itinerary is based on several conclusions. (1) First Corinthians 16:5-7 speaks of a change of itinerary. (2) Second Corinthians 1:15-16 reflects Paul's original plan, and 1 Corinthians 16:5-7 states his "Plan B." Paul, on or before his second visit, had spoken of a final double visit (2 Cor. 1:15-16) before he left for Jerusalem. The pain of his second visit caused him to stay away as long as possible, returning only after he passed through Macedonia (1 Cor. 16:5-7).[8] Others hold that Paul initially planned to travel to Corinth by way of Macedonia (1 Cor. 16:5-7), but later changed his journey to the double

6. For support of the second visit before 1 Cor., see Philip Edgcumbe Hughes, *Paul's Second Epistle to the Corinthians* (Grand Rapids: Eerdmans, 1962), pp. 31-33 (and p. 52 for other supporters); R. C. H. Lenski, *Second Epistle to the Corinthians* (Minneapolis: Augsburg, 1937), p. 799 (with somewhat less conviction, p. 14); D. Edmond Hiebert, *An Introduction to the New Testament* (Chicago: Moody, 1977), vol. 2, p. 111 (held tentatively); and Alfred Plummer, *A Critical and Exegetical Commentary on the Second Epistle of St. Paul to the Corinthians* (Edinburgh: T. & T. Clark, 1915), p. xviii, where he allows the possibility of the second visit prior to 1 Corinthians.
7. For a general survey of the chronology surrounding Paul's visits and letters, see Donald Guthrie, *New Testament Introduction,* 3d ed. (Downers Grove, Ill: InterVarsity, 1970), pp. 424-30.
8. Hughes, *Paul's Second Epistle to the Corinthians,* p. 32; R. C. H. Lenski, *The Interpretation of St. Paul's First and Second Epistles to the Corinthians* (Minneapolis: Augsburg, 1961), p. 14; Hiebert, *An Introduction to the New Testament,* 2:139.

visit plan of 2 Corinthians 1:15-16.[9] (3) If 1 Corinthians 16:5-7
was a change from the original double-visit plan, then Paul's
statement in 2 Corinthians 1:23, "I came no more to Corinth,"
meant that he had not been to Corinth since he wrote 1 Corinthians. A visit between 1 and 2 Corinthians would be excluded,
and Paul's second visit would have been made prior to the
writing of 1 Corinthians. That view of 1 Corinthians 16:5-7
and 2 Corinthians 1:23 produces the following order of events:
first visit; second visit; lost letter (1 Cor. 5:9); 1 Corinthians;
2 Corinthians; third visit.

THE OCCASION OF FIRST CORINTHIANS

After his second visit and follow-up letter (mentioned in
1 Cor. 5:9), several things happened in Corinth that caused
Paul to write yet another letter (1 Corinthians). Word reached
him through several avenues. Chloe's people reported that the
church had split into several factions, each claiming the
authority of a well-known figure: Paul, Peter, Apollos, or
Christ (1:12).

Some had become arrogant regarding Paul's return, which
he had promised during his second visit. (See the reference to
that promise in 2 Cor. 13:2.) They had misunderstood Paul's
letter about immoral associations and allowed an immoral
brother to fellowship with the Christian community (5:1-2).
Some asserted a superior wisdom, one that surpassed even
Paul's (4:7-10). Evidently, they felt that Paul's words carried
little weight (4:18). True, Paul said he would return with full
discipline (2 Cor. 13:2), but they were not convinced that he
had enough clout, to worry about his visit.

Not all was gloomy, however. The Corinthians were doing
generally well (1:47) and were worthy of praise (11:2). Paul

9. See, for example, C. K. Barrett, *A Commentary on the Second Epistle to
   the Corinthians* (New York: Harper & Row, 1973), p. 7; R. V. G.
   Tasker, *The Second Epistle of Paul to the Corinthians* (Grand Rapids:
   Eerdmans, 1958), p. 17; and Gordon D. Fee, "KARIS in II Corinthians
   I.15: Apostlic Parousia and Paul-Corinth Chronology," *New Testament
   Studies* 24 (1977-78), pp. 533-34.

also had, from his second visit, first-hand knowledge of their overall condition.

The Corinthians also sent a letter asking several questions, probably highlighted by the "now concerning" phrases throughout 1 Corinthians (7:1, 25; 8:1; 12:1; 16:1). The last question concerned the collection for the poor in Jerusalem (16:1-4). Titus had helped begin this work (2 Cor. 8:6, 10), and now the Corinthians needed to clarify some details.

Paul wrote 1 Corinthians during his two-year stay in Ephesus (Acts 19:1-10). The visitors from Corinth had arrived, as had the questions from the church. Paul had sent Timothy to remind the Corinthians of Paul's ways (4:17), and he expected him to return to Ephesus (16:10-11). Titus departed for Corinth, probably carrying 1 Corinthians, with orders to meet Paul in Troas.

Titus had been to Corinth in the past year to arrange the offering (2 Cor. 8:6, 10, 9:2), in which the Corinthians were willing to participate. If 1 Corinthians was written in the spring of A.D. 57 and 2 Corinthians in the autumn of the same year,[10] then these mentions of a preparation one year past put the date of Titus' work in A.D. 56. During that time, Paul was not only making preparations for the Corinthians' offering, but for one in Galatia as well (16:1). The offering for Paul's countrymen was a high priority and was part of Paul's conclusion of 1 Corinthians.

CONCLUSION

In addressing the Corinthian problems, Paul did not write all he could have. The Corinthians' specific troubles provided the grid by which he selected only the truths that would effectively speak to his readers. Just as Paul saw the targets for his truth, we must see them also in order to understand the letter of 1 Corinthians. Perhaps we will find similar targets in our own

10. Hughes, *Paul's Second Epistle to the Corinthians,* p. 33; Lenski, *Second Epistle to the Corinthians,* p. 14; Hiebert, *An Introduction to the New Testament,* 1:113, 147; Guthrie, *New Testament Introduction,* pp. 441-42.

lives that need to be pierced with the same arrows Paul shot so long ago.

OUTLINE

  I. Wisdom and the Cross (1:1—2:16)
      A. Greetings (1:1-3)
      B. Thanksgiving: Grace Given (1:4-9)
      C. Unity by Imitating Paul's Ways in Christ
         (1:10—2:16)
 II. Wisdom and Leadership (3:1—4:21)
      A. Paul's Past and Present Inability: The Corinthians
         "As Men" (3:1-4)
      B. The Correct Perspective on Leadership (3:5—4:5)
      C. Final Invitation and Appeal: Results of Being
         Apart From Paul (4:6-17)
      D. Arrogance in Paul's Absence (4:18-21)
III. Sexual and Social Purity (5:1—7:40)
      A. Judging Immorality in the Church (5:1-13)
      B. Use of Unbelievers (6:1-11)
      C. Relation of the Body to the Trinity and Immorality
         (6:12-20)
      D. Sex and Marriage: Staying or Changing (7:1-40)
 IV. Concerning Idols and Their Sacrifices (8:1—11:1)
      A. Introduction: Knowledge (8:1-3)
      B. The Effect of Knowledge Without Love (8:4-13)
      C. Why Paul Restricted Himself for the Weak and
         Ignorant (9:1-26)
      D. Past and Present Disqualifications (10:1-22)
      E. Application (10:23—11:1)
  V. The Traditions: Kept and Unkept (11:2-34)
      A. Praise for Kept Traditions: Women's Headcover-
         ings (11:2-16)

    B. No Praise for Unkept Traditions: The Lord's
       Table (11:17-34)
    C. Summary (11:33-34)
 VI. Spiritual Gifts and Love: Edification (12:1—14:40)
    A. The Source and Worth of Spiritual Gifts (12:1-31)
    B. The Better Way: Love (13:1-13)
    C. The Better Way Applied to Spiritual Gifts (14:1-40)
VII. The Question of the Resurrection (15:1-58)
    A. I Make Known the Gospel (15:1-2)
    B. Foundations of the Gospel (15:3-11)
    C. Implications of Denying Christ's Resurrection
       (15:12-19)
    D. Solidarity and Subordination Described (15:20-28)
    E. An Example and a Rebuke (15:29-34)
    F. Specific Questions About the Resurrection
       (15:35-49)
    G. All Must Change to Enter the Kingdom (15:50-57)
    H. Conclusion (15:58)
VIII. With a View to Paul's Future Arrival (16:1-24)
    A. The Collection (16:1-4)
    B. Paul's Itinerary (16:5-9)
    C. Timothy and Apollos (16:10-12)
    D. Closing Exhortations (16:13-18)
    E. Greetings from Aquila and Prisca and Paul
       (16:19-24)

2

WISDOM AND THE CROSS

(1:1—2:16)

INTRODUCTION

Though Paul dealt with many subjects in this long letter, the underlying concepts that guided him were few. In evaluating ideas that stretched from idol-sacrificed meat to the Lord's supper, from immorality to marital relationships, from spiritual gifts to travel plans, only one thought directed his conclusions—the cross of Christ. Each solution Paul presented came from his discernment of a problem's relationship to that great truth.

Paul's strategy was to state a problem and provide a solution. He also gave the purpose behind his solutions. The following statements highlight Paul's approach to the problem of leadership dealt with in his first four chapters, a unit of which chapters 1-2, our specific focus here, are the first part.

WORLDLY WISDOM AND LEADERSHIP FACTIONS

The problem.

> Now I exhort you, brethren, by the name of our Lord Jesus Christ, that you all agree, and there be no divisions among you, but you be made complete in the same mind and in the same judgment. For I have been informed concerning you, my brethren, by Chloe's people, that there are quarrels among you. Now I mean this, that each one of you is saying, "I am of Paul," and "I of Apollos," and "I of Cephas," and "I of Christ." (1:10-12)
>
> You are already filled, you have already become rich, you have become kings without us; and I would indeed that you had become kings so that we also might reign with you. (4:8)

The solution.

> Has Christ been divided? Paul was not crucified for you, was he? Or were you baptized in the name of Paul? (1:13)

> For Christ did not send me to baptize, but to preach the gospel, not in cleverness of speech, that the cross of Christ should not be made void. (1:17)

> For I determined to know nothing among you except Jesus Christ, and Him crucified. (2:2)

> But by His doing you are in Christ Jesus, who became to us wisdom from God, and righteousness and sanctification, and redemption, that, just as it is written, "Let him who boasts, boast in the Lord." (1:30-31)

> Therefore do not go on passing judgment before the time, but wait until the Lord comes who will both bring to light the things hidden in the darkness and disclose the motives of men's hearts; and then each man's praise will come to him from God. (4:5)

The purpose.

> Now these things, brethren, I have figuratively applied to myself and Apollos for your sakes, that in us you might learn not to exceed what is written, in order that no one of you might become arrogant in behalf of one against the other. (4:6)

The Corinthians had made premature evaluations of people and issues, evaluations that should have been left for the Lord at His day of judgment (4:5). Though some kinds of human judgment were necessary before the Lord came (e.g., 5:3), the Corinthians' problem was a wrong exercise of wisdom—a wisdom not of the cross but of their own inflated egos. Their faulty conclusions about their status as kingdom dwellers amounted to a final Day-of-the-Lord kind of judgment apart from the teachings of the apostles. That faulty position led to serious mistakes in all the other areas Paul dealt with in 1 Corinthians.

Behind those problems was a puffed-up attitude that if not

immediately stopped would have ruined much of the work in the church. As noted earlier, the word for arrogance was used in 4:6, 18-19; 5:2; 8:1; 13:4, and only again in the New Testament in Colossians 2:18.

In order to solve the problem of splits over leadership, Paul first focused his readers on the nature of their redemption in Christ (1:17—2:5). Then he revealed the nature and source of true wisdom and knowledge (2:6—3:4). Next he corrected their views on the time for and source of rewards (3:5—4:5). Finally he brought up their need to imitate him (4:6-17)—a touchy matter in view of their problems with falsely following human leaders.

STRUCTURE

The structure of the first four chapters alternates between facts from the Corinthians' situation and implications drawn out by Paul.

Facts (1:10-17):	their problem, Paul's actions
Implications (1:18-31):	God's method; wisdom and the cross
Facts (2:1-5):	Paul's actions; Christ crucified
Implications (2:6-16):	God's medium: the Spirit
Facts (3:1-9):	their problem, Paul's actions
Implications (3:10-17):	God's final evaluation of their work

Summary Exhortations (3:18—4:21)

GREETING (1:1-3)

THE WRITER AND A FRIEND ARE IDENTIFIED (1:1)

The "will of God" was central for Paul's directions to the Corinthians. (See the concept in 4:19; 12:18 and 15:38.) But that was a stock phrase in Paul's initial identification of himself in letters.[1] "Called" is shared with Romans 1:1. The

---

1. For a general introduction to the forms of Paul's letters, see William G. Doty, *Letters in Primitive Christianity* (Philadelphia: Fortress, 1973).

phrase "an apostle of Jesus Christ [or, *Christ Jesus*] by the will of God" is present in 1 Corinthians 1:1; 2 Corinthians 1:1; Ephesians 1:1, Colossians 1:1; and 2 Timothy 1:1. In addition to the longer introductory phrases noted above, the phrase "an apostle" or "an apostle of Jesus Christ" is present also in the openings of Romans, Galatians, 1 Timothy, and Titus. (Noteworthy are the introductions where Paul does *not* mention his apostolic credentials—Philippians and 1 and 2 Thessalonians.) Therefore, "by the will of God," while always an essential element of Paul's authority, was present in this verse as part of Paul's standard way of introducing himself.

The Sosthenes mentioned in Acts 18:17 was the Jewish leader of the Corinthian synagogue who was beaten before Gallio, the proconsul. There is no evidence that the Sosthenes of 1 Corinthians 1:1 was the same person mentioned in Acts. The name was not rare, being found in Greek letters and inscriptions.[2]

But the presence of a named individual in the greeting of Paul's letter must indicate that the readers knew of the person. It is on that basis that some link the Sosthenes of Acts and the one of 1 Corinthians. However, unlike the case of Timothy, we read nothing else about Sosthenes and therefore have no evidence to answer questions about his identity and relationship to Paul, the Corinthians, or the Christian ministry.

Though the identity of this Sosthenes escapes us, we must ask why he was mentioned alongside the apostle in the letter. What function did the co-writer play? Generally speaking, a co-writer indicated that the two authors had mutual interest in the letter's contents and, in agreement, had sent it under their collective names. Paul noted many people in the openings of his letters.

> Paul and Sosthenes our brother (1 Cor. 1:1)
> Paul and Timothy (our) brother (2 Cor. 1:1)
> Paul and all the brethren (Gal. 1:1-2)

2. James Hope Moulton and George Milligan, *The Vocabulary of the Greek Testament* (Grand Rapids: Eerdmans, 1930), p. 621.

Paul and Timothy (Phil. 1:1)
Paul and Timothy our brother (Col. 1:1)
Paul and Silvanus and Timothy (1 Thess. 1:1; 2 Thess. 1:1)
Paul and Timothy our brother (Philem. 1)

The list above shows that Paul commonly included someone else in his openings. Also, the concept of "brother" was common, even to the point of including "all the brethren" (Gal. 1:2). Therefore, the phrase "our [the Greek reads *the*] brother" was simply Paul's way of defining a friend named in his greeting. The result was more of a greeting than a list of the authors involved in the writing of the letter. Paul was always the central figure of authority in his letters. Those co-greeters, however, may account for Paul's tendency to switch from "I" to "we" at various points in his letters.

THE ADDRESSEES ARE IDENTIFIED (1:2)

Two things were noted here. First, the readers were sanctified in Christ. The way of sanctification was well known to them and was expanded in 1:4-9. The theme of calling unto sanctification occupied much of what Paul needed to say throughout the letter. (See 1:9 and 1:26 for the concept of calling.) But with all their faults, how could Paul call them sanctified? He could because he saw the whole picture of their position in Christ, not just their bad points. All the criticism that followed was given with the great truth of their calling and sanctification in mind.

Second, "in every place" was a technical expression (see 2 Cor. 2:14; 1 Thess. 1:8; and 1 Tim. 2:8) that Paul used to give a picture of the church in relation to a world-wide dependency upon Jesus as the commonly shared Lord (7:17; 11:16; 14:33). The Corinthians were related to a much larger group than just their own ingrown circle. That hinted at the problem Paul desired to correct—a narrow, self-centered religious outlook.

THE GREETING OF GRACE AND PEACE (1:3)

Though "grace and peace" was a common Pauline greeting,

it conveyed in a nutshell all the Corinthians needed to solve their problems. This greeting appears word-for-word in Romans, 1 and 2 Corinthians, Galatians, Ephesians, Philippians, and 2 Thessalonians. (Manuscript evidence also argues for the inclusion of "our" in 2 Thess. 1:2.) Colossians, 1 and 2 Timothy, and Titus vary only slightly from this pattern. Therefore, although the truth and power of this greeting are not diminished, it was not formulated specifically for the needs and problems of the Corinthians.

"Grace" was not to be taken abstractly or as a primary reference to the character of God alone. For Paul, grace was conceived only within the framework and definition of God's completed work through Christ. That grace would turn out to be the basis for correcting the Corinthians' inflated egos. All they had of any worth was graciously given to them by God in Christ (1:4-5). Notice Paul's pointed question in 4:7: "And what do you have that you did not receive? But if you did receive it, why do you boast as if you had not received it?" The only opposition Paul brought against their fleshly boasting was the practical implications of grace in their lives.

"Peace" resulted from wholeness of life brought about by receiving and appreciating grace. Most pointedly, the Corinthians needed unity with regard to their divisions over leaders. Community peace would only come through first realizing the nature of peace in each individual. That was Paul's starting point.

Thanksgiving: Grace Given (1:4-9)

Paul's thankfulness expanded the truth of God's grace and applied it to the Corinthians' problems. The first aspect of grace that Paul expanded was the source—given to them in Christ Jesus (1:4). Note the passive verb "was given." They had begun to think that *they* were the source of their gifts (see 4:7 and also chap. 12-14), and they needed to be reminded where their dependence lay.

Verse 5 shows how the grace mentioned in 1:4 was manifested: "in Him." The Corinthians were enriched in Christ, but, as 4:8 shows, they had misunderstood that to mean that they were already spiritually mature. Even so, Paul would not deny the richness of the effect of grace, though the Corinthians were confused about its source and use.

Note the repetition of "Lord Jesus Christ" in 1:3, 7-8, 10 (also 1:9, "Jesus Christ our Lord"). Paul continually stressed the role of Christ and God. The Father was the source of all gracious acts, and the Son was the means through which those acts were realized.

That functional relationship between the Father and the Son played more than a passing theological role in the letter. It formed the foundation for correcting various role problems that the Corinthians had concerning men and women, gifts and status, the resurrection, wisdom and leadership, and judgment of various sorts. God gave the grace, but He gave it within the character and mission of Christ. All giving from God was defined by Christ. The Corinthians, unfortunately, had developed other sources and definitions for grace.

But why did Paul single out the gifts of speech and knowledge (1:5)? He planned first to note the source of those gifts. Then, on that basis, he would draw out the implications not only for the Corinthians' incorrect use of speech and knowledge concerning the leadership factions, but also for all the other problems. Their basic problem concerned a misunderstanding of what true speech and knowledge were, and how they should be properly used.

"Even as" (1:6) further specified the results of grace being given (1:4) and the Corinthians being enriched in Christ (1:5), especially in speech and knowledge. The proof of that was the "testimony concerning Christ." Christ was among them, His presence evident by their speech and knowledge.

Verse 7 shows the result of the graciousness of God. They were "not lacking in any gift." (Note the fuller discussion of this fact and its misuse by the Corinthians in chapters 12-14.) But that statement did not stand alone. To it Paul added a statement to show the context for all of their gifts: an expectation of the end of the age.

Their gifts were an "awaiting time" phenomenon. The Corinthians were not yet at the end of their labors and were not yet filled or reigning in the kingdom (see 4:7-8). The placing of grace and the gifts of God into a temporary waiting period was foundational to the point Paul would make in 13:11. The Corinthians had not forgotten the goal of this age, the return of Christ. But they had forgotten the present-day implications of His return, and in doing so they had overestimated the worth, function, and point of their gifts.

Along with the temporal context for gifts, Paul added a statement that showed what God was doing during the awaiting period. "Who" (1:8) appears at first glance to refer to Christ, mentioned in verse 7. But the presence of "also" creates a problem with identifying the antecedent as the Lord. What had the Lord done that Paul could then add "also"? The continual referent who had done something was the Father, not the Lord. The Father had enriched them to the end, so that the presence of Christ among them was confirmed (1:6) and they lacked no gift (1:7). God *also* would continue the good work "to the end," to the very day of the Lord's judgment.

The end of 1:8 also indicates that two persons were in view; one who confirmed the day for another, the Lord.[3] How would this relate to the judgments being made in Corinth concerning leaders, purity, and so forth? The answer is seen in light of 4:5. The Corinthians were taking on the task of confirming who was and who was not blameless. But they were not qualified. Confirmation of character was the Lord's task alone. And the way to arrive at a blameless verdict on that day was not by human evaluations, but by the ongoing confirming work of God through His grace in Christ.

In verse 9, Paul made a general statement concerning the Father that reaffirmed what he said in 1:8: "God is faithful." Paul was speaking to solve problems, one of which was how the Corinthians perceived themselves and their leaders. Verse 9 pointedly exposed the foundation of their self-understanding.

---

3. F. W. Grosheide, *Commentary on the First Epistle to the Corinthians* (Grand Rapids: Eerdmans, 1953), p. 31.

All their hopes for religious success had to focus on (1) the judgment of the Day of the Lord, not on their present human evaluations of worth or blame; and (2) the Father's faithfulness to the ongoing process of confirmation. Paul centered their self-image and hope in the grace and faithfulness of God.

Therefore, 1:9 showed the certainty of 1:8, but it also pointedly prepared the way for discussion of the divisions in fellowship. Certainty was based on being kept in blamelessness to the end. Fellowship was based on the call of God to one Person: Christ. It was His church (1:2, "church of God"), and His church was called to fellowship with His son. That was not based on a mystical or exclusive experience, but was open to all Christians (1:9), a lesson many of the Corinthians needed to learn. In 1:4-9, Paul laid down the major truths he would apply to the problems throughout the letter.

UNITY BY IMITATING PAUL'S WAYS IN CHRIST (1:10—2:16)

SCHISMS AND THE CROSS INTERRELATED: DO NOT VOID THE CROSS (1:10-17)

Note the twofold use of "exhort" in 1:10 and 4:16. In 1:10, there is a command to unity (the repetition of "same," v. 10) of mind and judgment. That unity was the foundation for solving the problems. Though the Corinthians were richly gifted, they needed maturity in their thought and discernment.

Paul built his exhortation concerning divisions on the only source of unity, "the mind of Christ" (2:16). The way out of schism was a unified world view of Christ. "The name of our Lord Jesus Christ" (1:10) summed up all that had been explained in 1:1-9. The Corinthians had been called to fellowship with Jesus (1:9). Any fellowship around any other name was to nullify the cross of Christ. Notice in verses 13 and 15 how concerned Paul was that his name (or that of Cephas or Apollos) should be mentioned in the same breath with Christ's crucifixion or a believer's baptism.

Paul sought to accomplish unity in Christ by first describing the problem (1:11-16) through their behavior. They had frac-

tured into parties (1:11-12), as exhibited by their preferences
for certain human leaders. It does not appear that they were involved with doctrinal differences (except for the issue of the
resurrection in chap. 15). The way they spoke ("I am of Paul")
identified their fellowship not with Christ but with human beings. That maneuver amounted to a "cleverness of speech"
(1:17) that ended up voiding God's work through the cross.
The richness of God's gift of speech (1:5) had been turned to
exalting people, not God's Son.

The next section (1:13-16) developed the implications of
Christ, His cross, and His baptism. These teachings would
prove the only way back from their error.

When confronted with the problem of human parties, Paul's
God-given insight pierced to the heart of the matter—the implications of God's work through Christ (1:13a). What had
human beings to do with the Lord's redemptive death and the
fellowship entered into through baptism? They had forgotten
their identification with the crucifixion and the baptism into
Christ, and they had aligned themselves according to preferences for ministry styles. Individual leaders and their styles
were not to be the focus of fellowship.

Identification was elaborated upon next (1:13b-16). Were
they baptized into Paul? Verse 15 hints at the context: Someone claimed status because he was baptized in Paul's (or
Apollos's or Cephas's) name. Actually, few could be "identified" with Paul in that way (1:14-16). Paul stressed that he
came not to baptize but to preach the gospel (1:17a). The essential difference between preaching the gospel and baptizing was
identification. The Corinthians too easily tended to replace the
Lord of their salvation with the human instrument used to
bring them into the kingdom. Baptism was not meant to draw a
circle of followers around the human baptizer; rather, it should
have focused them on the Lord.

There does not appear to have been hostility between the
parties. But their wisdom had become the object of faith rather
than an occasion for understanding the cross. The object of
faith had become the "cleverness of speech" (1:17) and the

"wisdom of men" (2:5). That was equated with baptizing and the party spirit. The human personalities blurred the personality of God in Christ.

In verse 17, Paul referred in negative terms to the thrust and focus of his apostolic commission. He was not sent to baptize. He did not want to void the cross of Christ. By implication, the Corinthians were doing that very thing.

Paul did not say "void the gospel," because he wanted to focus on the specific implications of the cross of Christ. The Corinthians' problem needed that correction. Voiding the cross was the mistake that led the Corinthians into the errors of premature exaltation. Leaving the cross and the apostles behind, they falsely claimed to be reigning already (4:8). But the cross had to be their focus, because it was God's focus. The next section of the letter developed that theme.

The problem that voided the cross was that "cleverness of speech" cited in 1:17. That focus on speech formed the basis for 1:18—3:23.

THE WORD OF THE CROSS: REDEMPTION (1:18—2:5)

Paul was sent to preach the word of the cross. In 1:18—2:16, Paul told his readers why that message must not be voided: It alone brought the power of God in salvation. Why did the Corinthians not see that? In this section, Paul told them it was because they had adopted the ways of the worldly wise.

This section describes how people responded to the word of the cross. Two groups were in view, those who were being saved and those who rejected the gospel. Paul used the responses of those two groups to show the Corinthians' error. Though saved, they were using the wisdom of the world to evaluate their present standing in Christ—the very wisdom that God called foolish and that led the world's leaders to crucify the Lord. In 1:18-25, Paul showed what God did. The wisdom of men was viewed through the grid of the cross and found to be foolish and incapable of bringing redemption. The cross was viewed through the grid of worldly wisdom and found to be foolish. Paul's point is clear: Which wisdom would the Corinthians want to embrace?

In 1:26-31, Paul explained the reason for God's wisdom. The point of the Corinthians' calling was to allow them to participate in the redemption spoken of in 1:18-25.

In 2:1-5, Paul described his coming in weakness and wisdom. He explained why he was the vehicle for such a message of weakness and foolishness, and he showed how to escape from the circle of the perishing (1:18-25).

Two responses to the word of the cross (1:18-19). The word of the cross was the theme of this section. "For" (1:18) started the explanation of what it meant to preach in "cleverness of speech" (1:17) and why Paul absolutely rejected such a ministry. That was spoken in light of the responses of the two groups mentioned, "those who are perishing" and those "who are being saved." Those two groups arose because Paul wanted to build a case of identification. With whom would the Corinthians identify, the group who thought themselves wise but denied salvation, or those who might be called foolish by the world but were in reality wise unto God's salvation?

The "for" of 1:19 introduces scriptural support from Isaiah 29. The full Isaiah passage reads:

> Because this people draw near with their words and honor Me with their lip service, but they remove their hearts far from Me, and their reverence for Me consists of tradition learned by rote, therefore behold, I will once again deal marvelously with this people, wondrously marvelous; and the wisdom of their wise men shall perish, and the discernment of their discerning men shall be concealed. (Isa. 29:13-14)

How could something that seemed foolish to most people be salvation to a few? The answer was found in God's interpretation of Isaiah 29:14.

The point was not judgment on the wise but its implications for the church. Though the Corinthians' situation was not the same as that of those in Isaiah 29:10, 14, the correspondence was found in their world views. God would destroy the wise, or clever, wherever He found them, in B.C. Jerusalem or A.D. Corinth.

Where are the wise? (1:20-25). This was the first of two major questions Paul answered in the first part of his letter. The second was "What then is Apollos? And what is Paul?" (3:5). It was vital for the Corinthians to have the proper answer to those two questions, which also showed Paul's insight into the solution of that problem. They first needed to be taught about the end, in God's sight, of the world's wisdom. Then, in that light, they could be instructed about the proper view of Christian ministers who, above all, had the true wisdom of God.

Verses 20-31 are an initial development of the theme of "Where the wise?" from the perspective of salvation. Status and flashy speaking style aside, the only perspective of any worth to Paul was that of redemption. "But does it save?" was the only question central to Paul's interest. Where are the wise? They were made foolish in history. But how? By the divine saving of those who believe (1:21). Notice that in verse 21 Paul said "the message preached." The act of preaching was the catalyst for the hearers' salvation. That referred back to 1:17. Paul was sent not to baptize but to preach the gospel.

Another issue pertinent to the needs of the Corinthians was Paul's manner of introducing God's way of redemption in Christ (1:21). The wisdom of God came in such a way that the world in its wisdom did not come to know God, thereby excluding the knowledge of God from the worldly wise. That point was taken up later in chapters 2 and 3, where Paul had to say that the worldly wise Corinthians were not able to have the true wisdom and knowledge of God because of their carnality.

Verses 22-24 continue to place the wisdom and power of the cross in relationship to the responses of disbelieving groups, in this case Jews and Greeks. Note the parallelism in these verses. Those who seek signs stumble. Those who seek wisdom call the cross foolishness. But those who believe in Christ crucified find the power and wisdom of God.

"Christ crucified" (1:23) was how Paul characterized the

content of his preaching. But where was the resurrection and glorious ascension to the right hand of the Father?[4] Without doubt Paul wanted them to understand the heart of his message, the gospel, and the resurrection was central to the gospel, as chapter 15 clearly shows.

Why the emphasis on the cross then? Because Paul was not simply giving the content of the gospel in the abstract. He was relating that message to the specific problems of the Corinthians, in this case, a premature exaltation that voided the cross of Christ for the believer.

The only way out of that problem was to refocus the Corinthians on Christ crucified and the cross as the only model for the believer on earth. All Christians were called upon to take up their crosses and suffer with the Lord. Indeed, He was risen and ascended, but He had left the believer's exaltation for a future date. Until then, they were to understand that heaven was not gained if the cross was voided.

Verse 24 reintroduces the idea of calling (see 1:2). The called saw Christ and His cross as wisdom and power. No doubt the Corinthians would be agreeing heartily with Paul at this point. But Paul was just laying down foundational perspectives upon which he would draw some stinging principles to expose the Corinthians' errors (1:26-31; 3:1-4). Second Corinthians would show that not all in Corinth accepted the criticisms repentantly.

Why did Paul use paradoxical language in 1:25? Because of the implications of Isaiah 29:14. That was an effective and barbing way of speaking to the paradox of the Corinthians' life-style of "wisdom." Having been called according to the "foolishness" of God, why were the Corinthians involved with wisdom factions? God had called them in foolishness in order to shame and nullify the wise of the world. But the Corinthians were trying to reestablish respectability for what God had chosen to destroy by means of the cross of Christ.

Who became saved: redemption through foolishness

---

4. See E. E. Ellis, *Prophecy and Hermeneutics in Early Christianity* (Grand Rapids: Eerdmans, 1978), chap. 5 ("Christ Crucified"), pp. 72-79.

(1:26-31). This section begins in an explanatory way ("For"). Paul developed the Corinthians' own calling by keying off the mention of calling in 1:24. He aimed to establish God's focus for boasting. Here is a clear indication of the problem at Corinth. The readers were looking to the wise, mighty, and noble things of this world to find status in the church—the very things that were the opposite of the good pleasure of God in His own chosen way of salvation (1:21).

Verses 26-29 form a single sentence that was infused by Jeremiah 9:23-24, which is then partially quoted in verse 31. The similarity in thought is seen most clearly in the Greek translation of the Old Testament, and the entire quotation reads as follows:

> Thus says the LORD, "Let not a wise man boast of his wisdom, and let not the mighty man boast of his might, let not a rich man boast of his riches; but let him who boasts boast of this, that he understands and knows Me, that I am the LORD who exercises lovingkindness, justice, and righteousness on earth; for I delight in these things," declares the LORD. (Jer. 9:23-24)

The key words from Jeremiah are "wise," "might," and "rich." In 1 Corinthians 1:27-28, those terms are seen in Paul's contrasts between the wise, strong, and well-born on the one hand (1:26), and the foolish, weak, and poorly born on the other (1:27-28).

The idea that "God has chosen" controlled these thoughts and was used three times in 1:27-28. Why did God choose in that way? He did so in order to nullify the present order, with which the Corinthians were all too enamored (1:29). No flesh should boast before God. The contrast of verse 30 then becomes clear. Whereas some saw Christ as foolishness, He became "to us" wisdom from God. But Paul added more. Wisdom was not the only benefit of God's elective grace. The chosen received "righteousness and sanctification, and redemption" (1:30), all of which was "by His doing," not a result of the Corinthians' self-achievements. The purpose ("that," 1:31) behind God's originating all His great redemption in Himself was expressed in the terms of Jeremiah 9:23-24. All was from God in order that all boasting should center in the Lord. At present, Corinthian pride was being cloaked in a guise of wisdom. Christ no longer had the central hold on their thoughts and actions.

The quotation in 1:31 was taken from the message delivered by Jeremiah in the Temple gate. He had criticized Judah's cultic worship in Jeremiah 7, and in chapters 8—10 he had spoken of the future destruction of the Southern Kingdom. A call was given in Jeremiah 9:12 for the wise man to explain why the land perishes, but the answer was given instead by the Lord. The people had forsaken His law and were walking in their own ways. Jeremiah 9:23-24 was a summation of the call to the people that pointed them to the heart of the matter—not their own might, but the character of the Lord and His deeds were His delight.

In Jeremiah 9:23, the wise one was a subject repeated from Jeremiah 9:12. Paul saw that this was related to the problem at hand in 1 Corinthians 1. His use of the quotation formed the climax of his detailed elaboration of why God had chosen to act in the foolishness of the cross. God's reason was to make ineffectual the items and concepts (cataloged in 1:27-28) held high by unbelieving men. For the wise man in the last days of Judah and in first-century Corinth, the object of boasting remained the same.

Paul had several concepts in mind that had a determinative effect on this chapter. He concluded that pride was at the heart of the factions, that this pride was being cloaked in the guise of wisdom, and that the cross had lost its central hold on the Corinthians' thoughts and actions. Thus, the quotations in 1:19 and 3:31 were grouped around wisdom and boasting.

It is interesting to note that those were not mere word associations but were related to a consistent and preconceived historical framework of thought. The Old Testament context was quite appropriate, especially with regard to the words in Jeremiah 9:23 (in the Greek Old Testament). The method of moving from the concrete situation of the Old Testament to a universal principle was a legitimate and oft-seen Pauline method.[5]

What got them saved: the word of the cross (2:1-5). In 2:1-5, Paul corrected a misunderstanding about himself: he did not come in the wisdom of words (see 1:17). That returned to the ideas of wisdom and power (see 1:18). But most importantly, he introduced the concept of the mystery of God (2:1). The reading "mystery" (noted in the margin of the NASB) is to be preferred on the basis of the earliest manuscript evidence.[6] Immediately, Paul supplied what that mystery of God was. It was Christ crucified (2:2).

Christ crucified (see 1:17-18, 23) was the banner phrase for the Lord throughout chapters 1-14. It is only in chapter 15 that we find clear mention of the resurrected Lord. The vast weight of the letter fell on the significance of the cross, telling much about the problem of the Corinthians and the solution that occurred to Paul. Their premature exaltation had to be corrected by a refocus on the ongoing significance of the cross of Christ.

In 2:3-5, Paul showed his mode of preaching as well as its aim ("that," 2:5). He repeated the two key words from 1:18-31 regarding wisdom and power. Those were the two items some of the Corinthians felt must be present in any respectable apostle of Christ. By contrast, Paul was with them in "weakness and in fear and in much trembling" (2:3).

Paul's weakness and fear were not the result of his relatively unsuccessful ministry in Athens (Acts 17:32-34). Rather, he was describing how he ministered in any city. Paul spoke that way in 2 Corinthians 7:15, Ephesians 6:5, and Philippians 2:12. It was how he ordered his ways in humility and awe before God, rather than in the self-reliant and cocky manner of worldly wisdom.

The contrast in 2:4 was between words of wisdom and dem-

---

5. This will be seen again, for example, in 1 Cor. 10.
6. B. M. Metzger, *A Textual Commentary on the Greek New Testament* (New York: United Bible Societies, 1971), p. 545.

onstration of the Spirit and power. Power had already been
defined in 1:18 and 24. The only power Paul was concerned
with was that which saved by manifesting the truth of God in
Christ.

In that light, Paul spoke and acted so that the Corinthians'
faith would rest on the power of God, not on the wisdom of
men (2:5). But Paul said that not only to clarify his past
behavior. He also said it to provide a model for correcting the
Corinthians' tendencies to seek worldly wisdom. The important distinction was between the mode of the ministry and its
content. Paul's mode was in weakness, but his content brought
the power of God. The implications were clear. The Corinthians were involved in a life-style that could only build faith in
the wisdom of men and not in the power of God. Which would
they choose, flashy style or divine power?

REVELATION OF THE WORD OF THE CROSS: WHY SOME SAW IT
AND SOME DID NOT (2:6-16)

In 2:6-16, Paul outlined the problem that could block the
word of the cross in the unsaved and the saved. Paul had
already related how he came to Corinth and how he established
their faith in the power of God (2:5). Then, in 3:1-4, Paul
noted something that was denied to the Corinthians because of
their immaturity—the opportunity to minister to them as
mature people rather than babes.

Paul made that point by first showing why the rulers of the
age did not know God's wisdom: it was hidden in a mystery
(2:6-9). Then he showed who was able to receive the revelation
of God's wisdom: the spiritual person (2:10-16). Finally, he explained why the Corinthians were not able to be addressed as
mature people: they were fleshly (3:1-4). And, because they
were fleshly, they overlapped with the very group of "wise"
rulers whose false wisdom resulted in rejection of Christ.

That allowed Paul to explain how he could be mature, wise,
and spiritual and still be rejected and misunderstood. He
shared in the hidden mind of Christ that was above human

evaluation (2:15). That was a defense of Paul's integrity, though misunderstood, with a view to correcting the Corinthians. Three elements were under consideration: (1) the wisdom-mystery of God; (2) the ignorance of the rulers; and (3) the spiritual medium for knowing God's wisdom.

True wisdom (2:6-10). Paul first discussed what resulted from the divine wisdom's being hidden rather than available to anyone (2:6-9). Only the mature received that wisdom. This age and its rulers were passing away. Human rulers of this age had already been mentioned in 1:20 and 26 and related to the Corinthians' infatuation with their own little circles of ruling power. Also, the result of the rulers' "wisdom" was ignorance of God's true ways and the crucifixion of Christ (2:8). Paul could not escape from relating his argument to the crucifixion of Christ. For him, man's attitude toward Christ was dependent on his use of true wisdom, and that could only be equated with the pure word of the cross.

It is important to note that the wisdom of which Paul spoke was not in addition to the gospel. Paul did not contradict all he had said up to this point. Wisdom was only gained through the hearing and believing of God in the preaching of the gospel (1:21, 24, 30). Paul had already called the foolishness of the cross the wisdom of God (1:21), God's wisdom (1:24), and wisdom to us (1:30). The key term "mystery" had been applied in 2:1 to the message Paul proclaimed to the Corinthians.

It would seem, then, that when Paul mentioned a wisdom spoken "among those who are mature" (2:6), he had *receptivity* in mind rather than some kind of secret message. That is borne out by his carnal-spiritual exposition in 3:1-4. Therefore, Paul had already spoken the wisdom and mystery of God to the Corinthians. His point about speaking wisdom among the mature did not center on the *content* of wisdom but on one's *receptivity* to it.

"Among those who are mature" (2:6) equaled those who were spiritual and did not walk like "men" (3:1, 3). Notice the development of the identity of the mature. They were called mature (2:6); spiritual ones (2:13); not "natural," or carnal

(2:14); and again, spiritual ones (2:15; 3:1). The mature person's knowledge was the wisdom of God's ways in Christ, especially the cross. The truly spiritual and mature person was rooted in the word of the cross. But God had predestined that wisdom to result in "our glory" (2:7). That was the glory that came from receiving the "Lord of glory" (2:8). God had provided a way of true glory. Why did the Corinthians insist on the path of human glory and boasting?

The rulers, by contrast, heard the message of wisdom (2:8) but did not "accept the things of the Spirit of God" (2:14). Paul pointed out that the rulers of his age had no share in true wisdom, because it was embodied in a mystery from which the rulers were excluded.

Some expositors view those rulers as angels rather than men and find this confirmed by 1 Corinthians 15:24.[7] But Gunther Bornkamm asserts, in a study of Romans 13, that power and authority have a purely political meaning and are equivalent to earthly rulers. Those words only describe demonic powers with explicit additions in the New Testament.[8] Perhaps a combination of the two views is most appropriate for Paul's thoughts:

> By "rulers of this world" the Apostle appears to mean both the cosmic "principalities and powers" and also their actual human executives; and the very kernel of his doctrine of redemption is that by their tragic miscalculation the "rulers" became the instrument of their own destruction.[9]

On an earthly level, Paul had men like Pilate, Herod, and Caiaphas in mind (see Luke 12:11). The context also indicates

7. See Wilfred L. Knox, *St. Paul and the Church of Jerusalem* (Cambridge: University Press, 1925), pp. 112-13; and Walter Schmithals, *Gnosticism in Corinth,* ed. John E. Steely (Nashville: Abingdon, 1971), p. 137.
8. Gunther Bornkamm, *Early Christian Experience,* trans. Paul L. Hammer (London: SCM, 1969), p. 28, notes 36 and 39. That position is affirmed by Wesley Carr, "The Rulers of This Age—I Corinthians II.6-8," *New Testament Studies* 23 (1976), pp. 20-35.
9. G. H. C. MacGregor, "Principalities and Powers: The Cosmic Background of Paul's Thought," *New Testament Studies* 1 (1955), p. 23.

that human leaders who were ignorant of the plan of God through the cross were also referred to. That was why the rulers' ignorance of this mystery was demonstrated by their treatment of Christ (2:8). The rulers of this age would not have crucified Jesus if they had known. But they did not. In 2:9, Scripture explains why the rulers (or any human being) could not have known God's way of glory through the cross.

The precise location of the Old Testament passage or passages that Paul quoted in 2:9 has presented a continual problem for interpreters. Their conclusions may be classed under three headings: (1) they are from an extrabiblical source.[10] (2) They are of indeterminate origin. The second position is that the source of Paul's quotation is not recoverable. Ellis notes this as one of a group of passages that can be described as "merely quotations of substance whose source is conjectural."[11] (3) It is a free rendering of Isaiah 64:4. The third major position is that Paul broadly paraphrased the Isaiah passage.[12] It is noteworthy that in the classics, one finds that a purposely free quotation was a kind of "sign of mastery" over the source.[13] I conclude that Paul presented a free rendering of Isaiah 64:4.

The phrase "and which have not entered the heart of man" was an idiom that had been inserted into the Isaiah quotation.[14]

10. Joseph A. Fitzmyer, "The Use of Explicit OT Quotations in Qumran Literature and in the NT," *New Testament Studies* 7 (1960-61), p. 304; R. G. Hamerton-Kelly, *Pre-Existence, Wisdom, and the Son of Man. A Study of the Idea of Pre-Existence in the New Testament* (Cambridge: University Press, 1973), p. 114.

11. E. E. Ellis, *Paul's Use of the Old Testament* (Grand Rapids: Baker, 1957), p. 35. See also F. F. Bruce, *1 and 2 Corinthians* (London: Oliphants, 1971), p. 39.

12. Jean Hering, *The First Epistle of Saint Paul to the Corinthians,* eds A. W. Heathcote and P. J. Allcock (London: Epworth, 1962), p. 18; Archibald Robertson and Alfred Plummer, *A Critical and Exegetical Commentary on the First Epistle of St. Paul to the Corinthians* (Edinburgh: T. & T. Clark, 1911), p. 41.

13. Krister Stendahl, *The School of St. Matthew* (Uppsala: C. W. K. Gleerup, 1954), p. 157.

14. See Acts 7:23; Jer. 3:16; 44:21; 51:50; and J. B. Lightfoot, *Notes on the Epistles of St. Paul* (London: Macmillan, 1895), p. 176.

Stephen added the phrase to his quotation of Exodus 2:11-12 in Acts 7:23. Therefore, the phrase appears as a Semitic idiom that had come over into the Greek.

Verse 9 was designed to show that the rulers acted in accord ("just as") with what was written in Scripture, and that this action was a direct contrast ("but") to the condition supposed by verse 8. The quotation showed how all human entrances to God's hidden wisdom were blocked. His wisdom could not be seen or heard. It could not arise from within, in the heart's imaginations.

The point of this quotation was that God's wisdom was hidden to all but the mature, that His wisdom concerned the wonderful preparations of God in Christ, and that those preparations were only for those who loved Him. The knowledge of that wisdom would have kept the rulers from crucifying the Lord. But most importantly for the situation in Corinth, that wisdom would correct their tendency to follow after the patterns of worldly wisdom that ended in crucifying Christ and being blind to "all that God has prepared for those who love Him."

There is an interesting comparison to Paul's concepts in Matthew 13:14-15, which mentions Isaiah 6:9-10 in reference to seeing, hearing, and perceiving in the heart. In Matthew's gospel, Jesus was speaking concerning Israel's rebellious attitudes. Matthew displayed a division similar to Paul's between those the message of God was hidden from and those it was revealed to. Both Isaiah 6:9-10 (Matthew), and Isaiah 64:4 (Paul) were used to explain why the gospel was hidden from some and yet known by Christians.

Wisdom revealed: its means (2:10-16). After supplying the condition of the rulers' actions toward Christ in 2:8-9, Paul made known the medium through which the mystery was revealed: the Spirit. That both explained why the rulers did not know the wisdom of God and why it was possible for a believer to miss it. The only way anyone could have wisdom was through the Spirit, who was the only link to God's mind, and the only way to accomplish unity (1:10).

Verse 10 continued the thought of 2:6. There Paul said that he spoke a wisdom among the mature. Verses 8 and 9 showed the contrast of those who did not speak wisdom and qualify as mature. In 2:10-16, Paul explained ("for," 2:10) how a person matured and qualified to know God's wisdom. The Spirit was the vehicle ("to us") of the deep things of God.

The "for" of 2:11 introduced a parable of the human and divine spirits, and 2:12 applied that parable to those who were able to receive the message: the people of the Spirit. The contrast between the Spirit of God and the spirit of the world referred back to the groups mentioned in verses 6 and 7.

In 2:13, Paul returned to the spiritual group but elaborated on what he meant when he started this section with "Yet we do speak wisdom" (2:6). The manner of speaking was in spiritual thoughts matched with spiritual words. And all of that was matched up with spiritual people.

A question arises about who was referred to in these verses. Should we read "combining spiritual thoughts with spiritual words" or "interpreting spiritual things to spiritual men" (NASB margin)? The emphasis of this entire section is on who understood and received the wisdom of God. It spoke of reception rather than emphasizing the content of what was received. People, not data, were the issue:

> "We do speak wisdom among those who are mature" (2:6).
> "None of the rulers of this age has understood" (2:8).
> "For to us God revealed them through the Spirit" (2:10).
> "But a natural man does not accept the things of the Spirit of God" (2:14).
> "But he who is spiritual appraises all things" (2:15).

Verse 14 introduces the "natural man" to contrast with a spiritual person, and, in verse 15, Paul continued that contrast. Then Paul introduced yet another type of person, the fleshly man (3:1). The word used for "spiritual men" in 3:1 is the same Greek word used for "spiritual words" in 2:13. I would suggest, therefore, that 2:13 should also be translated "spiritual men."

In 1 Corinthians, Paul drew a contrast between the world's
and the Christian's ways of knowing. He stressed the Spirit as
the conveyor of God's wisdom. The thrust was to clarify why
men who were caught up in their own pride and boasting (a
description of the Corinthians, but tactfully focused on the rich
and powerful in the world) were ignorant of all the good that
God intended through Christ. Paul showed that the Christian
had a means of knowing God's mind (2:10-16).

By contrast, the unsaved person was totally unable to receive
God's Word (2:14). What the natural man could not appraise,
the spiritual man could (2:15), and because of that he was not
subject to human evaluation. That point was the basis for
remarks like those in 3:21-23; 4:3-5; and 9:3. Only the spiritual
were qualified to judge. To judge a spiritual person was to
judge the "mind of Christ" (2:16), a telling blow against the
Corinthians who were full of judgmental boastings.

Who was the spiritual person? He was the one who thought
like Christ (2:16). Here was the means to gain unity of mind.
Party spirit and divisions began because of the Corinthians'
faulty basis of evaluation. The quotation of 2:16 was taken
from Isaiah 40:13. That verse in Isaiah was part of a long section designed to display the surpassing greatness of God. The
answer to the question of Isaiah 40:18, "To whom then will
you liken God? Or what likeness will you compare with
Him?," was "No one." Though no one was comparable to
God, that awesome contrast was designed to encourage rather
than discourage, as Isaiah 40:29-31 showed.[15] The contrast was
to give the people unshakable confidence in God, to draw them
to Him. As men were confronted with their own inability to
direct God's Spirit and to counsel Him, they were brought to
the point of relying upon Him.

Paul's use of that passage implied the same as it did in
Isaiah, that no one knew the mind of the Lord or was able to
become His counselor. What follows the quotation is a slightly

---

15. See C. J. Labuschagne, *The Incomparability of Yahweh in the Old Testament* (Leiden: E. J. Brill, 1966), throughout.

adversative "but" (2:16*b*), indicating what was not true in the quotation was true of the "we" that followed. The Christian had been given the knowledge of God through the Spirit. That explained why no one appraised the spiritual person, and also explained the absurdity of presumptuous evaluations of men in Christ.[16] This is one of the strongest biblical statements of the believer's participation with and submission to God's thoughts.

Paul drew the principle that, apart from the Spirit, a person was not to presume to judge God's work among His people. More precisely, the gulf between the spiritual and the carnal was widely drawn. There could be no understanding of the former on the part of the latter; therefore, there could be no evaluation, either. Ability to judge the worth of Paul's ministry, for example, was directly related to one's receptivity to the mind of Christ in the Spirit. And that was where the Corinthians failed, as Paul shows in chapter 3.

16. Robin Scroggs, "Paul: SOPHOS and PNEUMATIKOS," *New Testament Studies* 14 (1967), p. 53.

3

WISDOM AND LEADERSHIP

(3:1—4:21)

BABES IN CHRIST (3:1)

In 3:1-2*a*, Paul described how he had to act with the Corinthians when he first came to them, as the spiritual person acted among the immature. Being confronted with their past spiritual denseness must have been a great shock for the Corinthians.

The language of mysteries (2:6-16) receded in favor of educational terminology. Paul's focus was on manner: "as," "as," "as . . ." (3:1). The Corinthians thought they were spiritual, but Paul noted that at the beginning they were immature and could not be addressed as spiritual men. That alluded back to "Yet we do speak wisdom among those who are mature" (2:6). At the beginning, the Corinthians were not mature; they were "men of flesh" (3:1).

But even in their immaturity, they had heard Paul proclaiming the mystery of God (2:1), and their response had brought the full gifting of God's Spirit (1:7). But the point of this section was not to discuss their strengths or weaknesses in doctrine or abilities. The point was to show their lack of spirituality. That explains how they, thinking that foolishness was wise and God's wisdom was foolish, had fallen into worldly-wise ways. They had not progressed beyond their beginning. Maturity did not just happen all by itself, it came only by continual conformity to the cross of Christ.

MILK AND SOLID FOOD (3:2-4)

The time when Paul could not speak to them as spiritual seems to be referred to in 2:1-5, the time of his original visit to Corinth. That visit had lasted for nearly two years (Acts 18:11, 18). Why, in all that time, had he not given them "solid food" (3:2)? Had he held out, or, as his critics might argue, did he just not have the insight?

In 3:2, Paul argued that he had limited himself for their good. "Milk" and "solid food" spoke first of the mode and secondarily of the content. Paul had spoken the mystery (2:1) and the wisdom of God (2:7), which was the same as the word of the cross (1:21, 23-24). But the mode related to how Paul ministered that wisdom to meet the Corinthians' needs.

In 3:2b, Paul exposed the problem. Though it was appropriate for the Corinthians to be immature and spiritually weak right after their conversion, the church at Corinth had continued in spiritual immaturity. Note the great emphasis ("indeed," "even") on the chronological aspects ("not yet," "now").

Paul then told them how he still had to act with them. Their inability was related to their nature ("fleshly," 3:3). The "still" of 3:3 and the "even now . . . not yet" of 3:2 show that the same condition still existed. Therefore, there is no significant difference between "flesh" (3:1) and "fleshly" (3:3). That failure to mature was the problem to which they were not facing up.[1]

Verse 3 explained that the difference between the spiritual and the fleshly was found in their behavior. "Fleshly" was closely aligned with "walking like mere men" (3:3b). It described a believer who at a particular point showed—in this case "jealousy and strife" (3:3)—no behavioral difference from an unbeliever.

---

1. *Flesh* (3:1) is used in Rom. 7:14; 2 Cor. 3:3; and Heb. 7:16. The word for *fleshly* (3:3) is found in Rom. 15:27; 1 Cor. 9:11; 2 Cor. 1:12 and 10:4; and 1 Pet. 2:11. Hans Conzelmann, in *1 Corinthians,* ed. James W. Leitch, (Philadelphia: Fortress, 1975), p. 72, sees no difference in meaning between the words.

"For" (3:3*b*) began an elaboration of the problem Paul had already mentioned in 1:10-11. Take a close look at "jealousy and strife." Those words uncover some key aspects of the setting at Corinth. The "I-am-of-my-leader" mentality was a result of interpersonal jealousy (the specifics are left unmentioned). From that jealousy over leadership arose public fighting and strife. The particulars of that strife will be seen in the upcoming problems dealt with in this letter.

In 3:4, Paul returned his readers to the point at which he had begun his solution to their problem of divisions in 1:10. "Mere men"—Paul had spoken much about men in 1:10—2:16. Human beings were the objects of God's great redemption in Christ (1:21). They also crucified the Lord (2:8). They were under God's judgment because of their false wisdom and true ignorance (1:19). Finally, they were to focus their boasting on the Lord (1:31), not on themselves (1:29).

But what had the Corinthians done? They had aligned themselves with the negative aspects of humanity. They were "mere men."

The Correct Perspective on Leadership (3:5—4:5)

Having shown them the mistakes they were making in judging, Paul turned to the question of who Paul and Apollos were.

In 2:6, "mature" meant perfect, or complete, in the sense of recognizing the source and control of the message, the Spirit. This section applied that definition to the Corinthians' problem with leadership preferences. The Corinthians had not understood the spiritual nature of the Body and therefore lacked discernment regarding the nature of the ministry. The ministry was not an ego game or a jockeying for status.

Paul then provided some "milk" conclusions ("What then," 3:5). How had the Corinthians been seeing themselves? They defined themselves by their alignment with particular human leaders (see 1:12 and 3:4). But Paul defined reward from the divine perspective. Human work that was not rewarded was the result of false wisdom—the very wisdom being fostered by the Corinthians.

SERVANTS, FARMERS, AND ARCHITECT (3:5-9)

Paul drew a conclusion ("What then," 3:5) in the light of his past and present inability to speak to the Corinthians as spiritual people. That conclusion exposed the true identity of Paul and Apollos, an identity the Corinthians should have known already.

"Servants" (3:5) pointed to a master. Did the Corinthians view their exalted leaders as mere servants? "Through whom" showed the leaders to be channels of God. The Corinthians had forgotten that they were not the source of their gifts (4:7), and they had made the same mistake in regard to their leaders.

"God was causing" (3:6) showed the leaders' dependency upon and limitation to Christ's gift. They were not self-sufficient workers for God. To sum up: Who were these great Christian leaders? Compared to God, nothing. In the church, any success was a gift ("the Lord gave," 3:5) from God alone.

Paul then used an illustration from agriculture (3:6), and verse 7 provided the moral. The figures of 3:6 derived from the "gave . . . to each" concept (3:5). Think about the reality behind the figures, and relate it to the concern regarding ministry. Paul said to boast only in the Lord (1:31) and throughout stressed that God was the source of their gifts. He now added the most powerful truth, that God caused the growth (3:7). All watering and planting would be futile if there were no growth.

Paul drove the point home with special reference to the Corinthians' problem with pride in their leaders (4:7). Who were Paul and Apollos? With growth in view, they were not *any-thing*. With the function of the leaders in view, Paul called them "servants" (3:5).

The unity of God's ministers was what one who walked according to men would miss. Because the Corinthians were trying to separate God's workers into status groups, they were splitting up their unity ("one," 3:8). Verse 8*b* shows that that unity did not blur personal responsibility for the servant. Each would receive his own reward.

The topic of reward stressed the final responsibility that was attached to the work of the ministry. "But each will receive his own reward according to his own labor" was a parenthetical remark anticipating 3:10-17. The "for" of 3:9 returned the thought to an explanation of 3:8a: "Now he who plants and he who waters are one." But outward success was not the basis of reward. The true standards of what made one's ministry rewardable ("according to his own labor" [3:8]) would be explained in 3:10-17.

Note the threefold mention of God in 3:9. The workers and the congregation were not to be viewed apart from being God's. That was a direct correction of the Corinthians' ways of viewing themselves as belonging to men (Apollos, Cephas, Paul). "Field" related to the previous images, and "building" provided a transition to the argument that follows.

REWARD AND EVALUATION DEVELOPED: DAY OF FIRE (3:10-17)

This section spoke in more detail to the problem of judging the quality of people's ministries. That problem precipitated the leader preferences in chapters 1 and 2 and the judging of faithfulness in 4:1-6.

Paul moved from agricultural to architectural metaphors ("building," 3:9b) and elaborated two ways of building. That provided wisdom so that he could be a "wise master builder." Paul continually stressed that his ministry was an effect of God's grace, not of his own talents and abilities, so that the Corinthians could realize who their leaders were.

A "wise master builder" did not just sit in his office and design buildings. He was one who both designed (as master) and worked (as a builder) on location. The same word was used in the Greek Old Testament version of Isaiah 3:3.

Paul's mention of a master builder and other builders ends with the command to watch out. But who was being warned in 3:10c? The builders (3:10b). The focus moved beyond Paul and Apollos to the others who were building upon the foundation. That introduced a problem: what was one to be careful about as he built? The next verse, 3:11, supplied the reason why they should watch out, and elaborated on the ideas of the cross and baptism mentioned in chapter 1.

The reason one had to be careful when building on the foundation was that the foundation was a Person, not a thing (3:11). Laying that foundation was not merely the transmission of a body of doctrine or behavior; rather, it meant carefully involving a person with the very life of Christ. "The one which is laid" referred to the great power of God through Christ on the cross. Their "I-am-of-Paul" mentality cut across and voided that great foundational act of God in Christ.

"Now if" (3:12-13) began a description of the quality of the building. Note the stress on "each" (twice in 3:13 and also in 3:8). The Day of the Lord, not human evaluation, would show the quality. Verse 12 took the concept of building from verse 10 and elaborated upon the meaning of care in building. Two figures of quality were pictured; "gold, silver, precious stones," and "wood, hay, straw." Those figures stressed both the mode of the building process ("how he builds" [3:10]) and the result.

It is important to note that secret work was not in view. How else could someone know what he was building if its nature would only be revealed at the last judgment? The work was observable to Paul and the other builders. Quality could be known now, but reward was God's business alone (3:13). Here was the final evaluation of the work with regard to reward. The repeated phrase "If any man's" (3:14-15) introduces the basis for reward (see 3:8). Reward, not salvation, was the issue (3:14-15). The concept of foundation and building led Paul's thoughts to the center of God's presence with the Corinthians, and to the center of their problem. They thought they were spiritual, but they were not (3:2*b*-4). And now they were in danger of an error that could go beyond the "saved, yet so as through fire" (3:15) judgment and into eternal destruction. The issue went beyond leadership preferences and carnal behavior. It was building that destroyed the temple of God.

Destruction here can only be defined with reference to the preceding context, a building process that was destructive of the foundation's original purposes. Paul did not elaborate on his meaning. His purpose was to bring up the possibility of wrecking God's desires for the holiness of His church by worldly wisdom and its ensuing eternal destruction. That threat should have caused them to pay attention to the next exhortation.

DO NOT BE DECEIVED CONCERNING WISDOM, AND THEREFORE
DO NOT BOAST IN MEN (3:18-23)

In light of the serious facts mentioned in 3:16-17, Paul warned them not to be deceived. That returned to the earlier themes of the wise, this age, the fool (defined in 1:20), and boasting. Chapter 3, verses 18-21*a,* summarized chapters 1-2, and 3:21*b*-23 summarized 3:1-17.

In the first part of chapter 3, Paul showed that because of their factious spirit the Corinthians were unable to receive the teaching of the mature. That spirit was especially ill-grounded because the human objects of boasting were, in fact, unified in their efforts (3:8). Thus, the distinctions were superfluous. Verses 10-17 presented a double-edged warning to those who perverted Paul's teaching.

Paul showed that the Corinthians' immaturity kept them from understanding the nature of God's work and moved them away from the foundation of their faith. They were the temple of God and should, therefore, have understood all their attendant responsibilities. But self-deception (3:18), not doctrinal matters, was at the core of their problem. That was a plain call for self-appraisal. The deception centered on the nature of the builders and the building. Verse 18 began Paul's summary exhortation that the wise of this age should become foolish—that is, truly wise by God's standards.

"For" (3:19) reintroduced and reinforced the previous thoughts from chapters 1 through 3 by quotations of Job 5:13 and Psalm 94:11 (3:20). Self-deception did not deceive God (3:19-20). The specific context of Job, the prelude to Eliphaz's exhortation in Job 5:17, concerned how God would lift up the lowly and confound the evildoer.

Psalm 94 was a curse against the enemies of God. The wicked were described in Psalm 94:1-6. Psalm 94:7 then supplied insight into the thoughts of the wicked, and it also acted as the basis for verses 8-11. In response to the accusation that the God of Israel did not pay heed, the wrongdoers were themselves told to pay heed and realize the true identity of the God they were mocking. God, who made the ear and eye, heard and saw better than they. In contrast to the thoughts of the One who was the source of knowledge, man's thoughts were like a vapor.

Paul changed the "men" in the psalm to "wise" in order to make the quotation more applicable. That was not proof-texting on Paul's part, because he did not violate the essential historical understanding of the Old Testament text or apply it to a situation beyond its limits. Here was what already had been seen in 1 Corinthians 2:16, the application of general principle to a specific situation.

The quotations of 3:19-20 were followed by the exhortation not to boast in men (3:21*a*). To that was an added encouragement that in Christ all belonged to them; hence, no need to seek the security of partisan favor in men should arise (3:21-*b*-23).

"So then" (3:21) introduced a caution not to boast in men, the problem only hinted at up to this point. Here we see why Paul spoke about boasting before God (1:29) and boasting in the Lord (1:31), and why he defined himself by his weakness and trembling (2:3). Now we also see why Paul was led to speak so much about the cross of Christ and the world's reactions to it. The Corinthians were boasting in men.

The high point of Paul's thoughts on the problem of divisions ended with the focus on God. The Corinthians would not have included 3:23. They also would have agreed with 3:21*b* but would not have seen its implications until this point in the letter. All things belonged to them, so why did they settle for just a part (human leaders), and an insignificant part (3:7) at that?

THE QUESTION OF FAITHFULNESS: GOD ALONE JUDGES IT (4:1-5)

In 4:1, Paul continued to answer the questions of 3:5: "What then is Apollos? And what is Paul?" Paul repeated the same answer from 3:5, "servants of Christ." But he added "stewards of the mysteries of God." That addition collected the thoughts of 2:7, 12. The idea was one who handled God's affairs.

"Stewards" described one who was the chief steward but who also worked with his hands. Paul was a servant of Christ to bring redemption to the Corinthians, but he was also entrusted with the mysteries of God.[2] He was mature and wise in God's sight, if not in the Corinthians'.

But Paul's thoughts were on the Corinthians' problem of falsely evaluating leaders. Chapter 3 ended with all belonging to God. Therefore, since both the Corinthians and their leaders belonged to God alone, the question of evaluating service must be left to Him alone. So Paul's thoughts turned to *how* he was being evaluated. Consider us, Paul said, but do not put the final price tag on us.

In that light, the question of faithfulness came up (4:2) as the Corinthians played their "who is the best leader" game. They judged (4:3, 5) by their own standards. That related to the judging theme of 2:15-16 and to the reward themes of 3:8 and 13-14. In 2:15-16, the issue was the wisdom or foolishness of the gospel. In 4:3, the issue was judgment based on faithfulness.

In chapters 2 and 4, Paul stressed that he was not subject to human judgment. It was a "very small thing" for Paul to be judged by the Corinthians or even himself (4:3). Why was that? Because there was only one Judge, the Lord (4:4), and He alone had perfect judgment. That related back to Paul's words on the judgment of the Lord in 3:12-23. Even if Paul found nothing against himself, he still knew that God alone could

---

2. William L. Lane, "Covenant: The Key to Paul's Conflict with Corinth," *Tyndale Bulletin* 33 (1982), pp. 3-29.

render the accurate and final evaluation of his ministry. That lesson was sorely needed by Paul's readers.

Paul told them not to judge before the Lord's time of evaluation and praise. Though the Corinthians were probably not aware of it, their judgment had taken on the finality of evaluation appropriate only for the Lord at His day. They had written off some leaders (and fellow believers) and had given the seal of approval to others. So in 4:1-5, a final kind of judgment was in view, a final tag of approval or rejection. Of course Paul did not hesitate to praise (11:2) or not praise (11:17) his people. But the judgment being made by the Corinthians here was a non-ministry judgment based on criteria that cut across God's purposes in the cross.

A conclusion ("Therefore") was made in 4:5. The Lord would come to judge—anything else was "before the time." At that time the Lord would do two things that were beyond the Corinthians' abilities to evaluate. He would "bring to light the things hidden" and "disclose the motives of men's hearts." Then and only then could "each man's praise" be given "from God." Who could judge the considerations of the hearts? God alone. But the Corinthians had foolishly assumed that prerogative.

FINAL INVITATION AND APPEAL:
RESULTS OF BEING APART FROM PAUL
(4:6-17)

ABOVE WHAT IS WRITTEN (4:6-13)

In 4:6, Paul summed up all he had written in 1:10—4:5 ("these things"). "Figuratively applied" referred to the many images used by Paul to make his point: Paul was not crucified for them or the source of their baptism (1:13); planting and watering (3:6); God's fellow-workers (3:9); wise master builder (3:10); servant (4:1); and stewards (4:1). Those figures showed Paul and Apollos in their proper light—channels of God's power through the gospel. That related to the fact of the Corinthians' being puffed up and exalting themselves over the Word.

The purpose ("that," 4:6) was to teach a lesson. The Corinthians had exceeded what was written. Paul had spoken of leaders in order to show the followers their proper place. Their exceeding "what is written" had led to arrogance and all its ensuing problems as seen in 1 and 2 Corinthians. The words "exceed" and "in behalf of" translate the same Greek word. That Greek word has the sense of "over." To go over what was written resulted in their becoming arrogant over each other. One led to the other, and Paul wanted it stopped.

Morna D. Hooker presents a more specific focus for "what is written."[3] She argues that the phrase referred to the two quotations in that section from Job and Psalms (3:19-20). But one ought also to look at the four quotations in chapters 1 and 2. Hooker further argues that going above what was written was being fostered by some in the community. Examples could be drawn from the matter of immorality in chapter 5, litigation in chapter 6, and the problems with women's head coverings in chapter 11.

Clearly the Corinthians had become "arrogant in behalf of one against the other." That arrogance is seen throughout the letter (4:6, 18-19; 5:2; 8:1).

Paul's sarcastic frontal attack in 4:7-13 had been prepared for by chapters 1-3. His questions in 4:7-8 uncovered the root problem in Corinth. Answer each question in 4:7 in the light of the first three chapters. Who regarded the Corinthians as superior? Only themselves. What did they have that they did not receive? Nothing. Then why did they boast? Because they were foolish and acting like worldly people.

The sarcasm continues in 4:8 by means of three images: filled, rich, and kings. The Corinthians acted as though all earthly problems were behind them, as if they were already in the kingdom to come. Although that would be true some day,

---

3. " 'Beyond the Things Which Are Written': An Examination of I Cor. IV. 6," *New Testament Studies* 10 (1963-64), pp. 127-32.

they were being premature. They had left out God's coming judgment (4:5).[4]

Worst of all, they had ignored Paul's model of humility and entered their "kingdom" without him. A poignant word in this section is "without" (4:8). That is the key to the context of 1:10—4:17 and to the lesson to be learned "in us" (4:6).

Paul ended the sarcastic rebuke in 4:8b. How nice it would have been for the reigning Corinthians to allow Paul to reign with them.

In 4:9-13, Paul showed where the Corinthians went "without" the apostles. He reflected the real world—there was no reigning yet. He first described his lot in life and then the Corinthians'. They, however, had not followed Paul's way. They were above that.

In verses 11-13, Paul listed conditions that were despised by the world. Did the Corinthians despise the same things? Paul's "we are . . . but you are" litany in verse 10 could only have been received as a stinging blow to the puffed-up group. But Paul was not talking about himself to garner sympathy or to lash out. He spoke to minister.

PAUL AS FATHER, NOT SHAMER (4:14-15)

Paul's unique paternal relationship with the Corinthians provided a buffer and corrected any thoughts that Paul said those things to shame them. Also, it provided the context for the options mentioned in 4:21.

"Shame" (4:14) equaled the worldly way. "Admonish" equaled the ministry of the Word and Spirit. That stressed the manner of how Paul spoke to them. His attitude and feeling when addressing them was always ministry. If there ever was a severing of warmth in relationship and goodwill, it would never come from Paul's side. (See the expansion of that in 2 Corinthians 6:11—7:2.)

---

4. Anthony C. Thiselton, "Realized Eschatology at Corinth," *New Testament Studies* 24 (1977-78), pp. 510-26.

Many tutors could not equal a father (4:15). The concept of "tutor" was a guardian, not a father. But Paul was not merely being sentimental. He carefully defined his paternal relationship: "in Christ Jesus" and "through the gospel."

IMITATE PAUL'S UNIVERSAL WAYS (4:16-17)

"Be imitators of me" (4:16-17; for "I exhort you, brethren," see 1:10). That was a risky command in light of the problem concerning the group ("I am of Paul") mentality.[5] Though Paul hoped to come to Corinth soon (4:19), his love for the Corinthians could not wait. He made two attempts to help the Corinthians; a personal visit from Timothy (4:17), and this letter, both of which were stop-gap measures until he could arrive.

But Paul's ways were not idiosyncratic. They were "in Christ" and universally laid down (see 1:2; 11:16; and 14:36). They were consistent everywhere. Later he said that to imitate him was to imitate Christ (11:1). What were the specific ways Paul wanted them to imitate? (1) Their ministry should further the cross, not void it (1:17). (2) They should boast in the Lord, not men (1:31). (3) They should ground people on the power of God, not the wisdom of men (2:5). (4) They should build a ministry that matched Christ, the foundation (3:10-11). (5) They should live for the Lord's evaluation, not for their own or others' (4:4). (6) They should seek to correct each other by admonishment, not shame (4:14).

Clearly, Paul's method was to see everything in relationship to Christ. Then Paul worked out the implications of that: in the case of the Corinthians, their boasting in human beings.

ARROGANCE IN PAUL'S ABSENCE (4:18-21)

In 4:6, Paul noted that the Corinthians had a problem with arrogance. He did his best to correct their boasting in human

5. Boykin Sanders, "Imitating Paul: 1 Cor. 4:16," *Harvard Theological Review* 74 (1981), pp. 353-63.

leaders. Now he had to deal point by point with the specific disasters arrogance had spawned.

NOW, AS TO *ME* NOT COMING (4:18)

Timothy had probably arrived in Corinth. This letter was on its way. But some in Corinth continued their arrogant ways as if their spiritual father would stay away forever. That sounds a bit like "When the cat's away. . . ." Paul's opponents dared him to show his face. That was exactly the situation reflected in 2 Corinthians. In significant ways the situation only got worse after 1 Corinthians was received.

"Arrogant" (4:18) repeated a key word to the whole context of 1 Corinthians, as we saw in chapter 1 of this text.

I WILL COME SOON: WORD OR POWER (4:19-20)

Paul made a distinction between "words" and "power" (4:19). What power would he show? Paul defined the distinction between word and power around the nature of the "kingdom of God" (4:20). In 4:8, the Corinthians were already reigning in a kingdom of their own making. They were reigning, but on whose terms? Undoubtedly they would have argued that it was God's kingdom. But Paul knew better. His kingdom consisted in the accomplishment of the will of the King, not in words from carnal believers.

The kingdom "consists" in power. Paul would not come in word, because ("for," 4:20) the kingdom was not in word. Far from some kind of physical duel, Paul spoke of kingdom power here the way he had been speaking of it since the start of this letter. Kingdom power was the presence of the Spirit for gifting (1:7) and the effecting of salvation (1:18, 24). Most importantly, see 2:4-5:

> And my message and my preaching were not in persuasive words of wisdom, but in demonstration of the Spirit and of power, that your faith should not rest on the wisdom of men, but on the power of God.

Power, in this context, was what accomplished God's redemption in Christ.

PAUL'S CERTAIN COMING (4:21)

Paul gave his readers a choice. They could receive Paul's love, or his rod. "Rod" (4:21) was a figure for Paul's verbal discipline whereby he would judge their standing and make his verdict. Read 2 Corinthians 13:2-5:

> If I come again, I will not spare anyone, since you are seeking for proof of the Christ who speaks in me, and who is not weak toward you, but mighty in you. For indeed He was crucified because of weakness, yet He lives because of the power of God. For we also are weak in Him, yet we shall live with Him because of the power of God directed toward you. Test yourselves.

The issue of Paul's power was linked to his fidelity to the faith and Christ's presence in him. Paul turned the tables and applied the question of power and Christ's presence to the Corinthians.[6] Paul's second visit preceded the writing of 1 Corinthians; therefore, they had already heard these words when Paul wrote 1 Corinthians 4:20. Power was the proof of who conformed to the truth of God in Christ.

Paul gave them two options: love or a verbal spanking. That set the scene for the tone of this letter—trying to solve the problem through a letter before Paul had to arrive. Actually, he delayed his arrival so that when he did finally arrive, he would not have to fight (see 2 Cor. 1:23—2:1). Paul asked what they desired, a rod or love. After the first four chapters of this letter, could they doubt which option Paul desired?

6. See Robert B. Hughes, *Second Corinthians* (Chicago: Moody, 1983), pp. 135-39.

4

SEXUAL AND SOCIAL PURITY

(5:1—6:20)

INTRODUCTION

Chapters 5 and 6 are part of a larger section that includes chapter 7. All three chapters are concerned with how individual purity affected the community. The emphasis moves from sexual purity (5) to social purity (6:1-11), then back to sexual purity (6:12—7:40).

THE SINNING BROTHER (5:1-13)

The problem.

> It is actually reported that there is immorality among you, and immorality of such a kind as does not exist even among the Gentiles, that someone has his father's wife. And you have become arrogant, and have not mourned instead, in order that the one who had done this deed might be removed from your midst. (5:1-2)

The solution.

> I have decided to deliver such a one to Satan for the destruction of his flesh, that his spirit may be saved in the day of the Lord Jesus. (5:5)

The purpose.

> Clean out the old leaven, that you may be a new lump, just as you are in fact unleavened. For Christ our Passover also has been sacrificed. (5:7)

LETTING UNBELIEVERS DECIDE LEGAL MATTERS (6:1-20)

The problem.

> Actually, then, it is already a defeat for you, that you have
> lawsuits with one another. Why not rather be wronged? Why not
> rather be defrauded? On the contrary, you yourselves wrong and
> defraud, and that your brethren. (6:7-8)

The solution.

> All things are lawful for me, but not all things are profitable. All
> things are lawful for me, but I will not be mastered by anything.
> (6:12)

> Or do you not know that the unrighteous shall not inherit the
> kingdom of God? . . . but you were washed, but you were sanc-
> tified, but you were justified in the name of the Lord Jesus
> Christ, and in the Spirit of our God. (6:9*a*, 11)

IMMORALITY

The solution.

> Do you not know that your bodies are members of Christ? Shall I
> then take away the members of Christ and make them members
> of a harlot? May it never be! (6:15)

> Or do you not know that your body is a temple of the Holy Spirit
> who is in you, whom you have from God, and that you are not
> your own? (6:19)

JUDGING IMMORALITY IN THE CHURCH (5:1-13)

Chapter 5 may appear to begin abruptly, but the thought is
closely tied to the ending of chapter 4. Chapter 4 ended with
Paul's giving the Corinthians a choice: he could come in wrath
or in love. That wrath was related to the arrogance of some
(4:18) concerning his return.

The specific Corinthian arrogance was mentioned in 4:6.
Splits over leaders led to arrogance against each other, with the

result that some could not have cared less about Paul's return or his authority. Chapter 5 deals with the first of several aberrant results of that community arrogance. Paul used several terms to correct that problem: "remove" (5:2, 13), "deliver . . . to Satan" (5:5), and "clean out" (5:7).

ARROGANT IN THEIR SIN (5:1-5)

The sin concerned a stepson and his stepmother. "His father's wife" (5:1) was an Old Testament and rabbinical term for stepmother (see Gen. 35:22; 49:4; 2 Sam. 16:22; 20:3; 1 Chron. 5:1). Marriage to a stepson was forbidden by Jewish and Roman law.[1]

The Corinthians' response to that sin was puffed-up boasting (5:2). That indicated an established and continuing state of pride. The first manifestation of that arrogance had been leadership factions (chap. 1). But here we find a more sinister manifestation—the inability to see sin as sin, and the resultant attempts to justify living with it.

The mourning of which Paul spoke (5:2) was not sentimentality but rather an emotional reaction to the awfulness of sin strong enough to result in the removal of it. The Corinthians problem would have gone something like this. Someone would have said, "That man should be removed from our fellowship. He's sinning." But another would respond, "Don't worry about it. We can live with it."

Paul had already judged this man (5:3), but for what reason? Though Paul was certainly concerned about community purity, he had not forgotten about the offender. He desired the punishment to have a good effect: to save the person in the day of the Lord (5:5). Paul's response was an abiding, long-distance judgment. In view was the Corinthian church assembled in order to excommunicate the offender. Paul would be there in spirit, in the judicial power of the Lord (5:4).

"Deliver such a one to Satan" (5:5) embodied the corporate

1. Hans Conzelmann, *1 Corinthians,* ed. James W. Leitch (Philadelphia: Fortress, 1975), p. 96.

(Paul and the assembled Corinthian church) human response to sin—removing the evil from the fellowship. Paul used several other terms for the same thought ("Clean out the old leaven" [5:7]; no association with an immoral brother [5:11]; "Remove the wicked man" [5:13]).

Besides purity of the church, the purpose of that removal was "the destruction of his flesh" (5:5). Some see "flesh" to be very similar to "body" (5:3), so that Paul spoke of the man's physical destruction.[2] Conzelmann and Barrett argue that "destruction" was too strong to mean anything less than death. Hope for the man's salvation rested only on the final events of the Day of the Lord. "Flesh" is best interpreted, therefore, as nearly synonymous with "body" (5:3; 15:38-39).[3]

Elsewhere, Paul used the concept of destruction for the devastation at the Lord's return (1 Thess. 5:3), for eternal destruction (2 Thess. 1:9), and for the results of sin in this life (1 Tim. 6:9). The usage in 1 Timothy 6:9 is most similar to Paul's thoughts here. The offender would be subject to earthly destruction at the devil's hands, possibly even to physical death. But the physical judgment is not to be seen as the cause of the man's salvation.

The judgment of God was corrective ("that his spirit may be saved"). "Destruction of his flesh" leaves two possibilities open: correction for his fleshly behavior in this life, or cessation of his ways by death.[4] That did not mean that, if allowed to continue, the man might have lost his salvation. Rather, it meant God could end the man's sin by corrective suffering or

2. Conzelmann, *1 Corinthians*, p. 97, calls "flesh" and "body" synonyms; C. K. Barrett, *A Commentary on the First Epistle to the Corinthians* (London: Adam & Charles Black, 1973), p. 126, believes that destruction of the flesh meant physical death, though it is not clear how that would effect the offender's salvation.

3. See F. W. Grosheide, *Commentary on the First Epistle to the Corinthians* (Grand Rapids: Eerdmans, 1953), pp. 123-24; and also R. C. Lenski, *The Interpretation of St. Paul's First and Second Epistles to the Corinthians,* (Minneapolis: Augsburg, 1937), pp. 215-18, for the position that sees a distinction between flesh and body.

4. Anthony C. Thisleton, "The Meaning of SARX in I Corinthians 5:5: A Fresh Approach in the Light of Logical and Semantic Factors," *Scottish Journal of Theology* 26 (1973), pp. 204-28.

by ending his earthly life so that, at the very least, his life could resume in the Day of the Lord. This is similar to God's judgment on those who abused the Lord's table (11:29-31); some were sick, but some were dead.

Such potentially drastic action was not a snap judgment on Paul's part. The act occurred and was allowed to continue. No doubt much debate went on in Corinth over the matter. Then word reached Paul, and he considered the correct response to it.

BOASTING IN EVIL (5:6-8)

The Corinthians had boasted in men (3:21). Here they boasted in sin. They thought they were so strong (4:8) that they could live with it. But Paul once again directed their attention to the true implication of their "freedom" to live with sin—they could become sinners themselves. Their boasting was caused by their puffed up state (5:2). Some raised a question in Corinth about what was "good" (5:6; 7:1). Their boasting was not good—though some evidently argued it was—because it opened them up to evil.

The leaven proverb (5:6*b;* see Gal. 5:9) introduced Paul's main thought: a little evil could infect the whole community of Christ. Once again, Paul saw the implications of the Corinthians' actions for their life and redemption in Christ. The idea of leaven did not come from the bake shop but from the Passover, the great saving event of Israel that had become the central image of Christ's redemption. The command to clean out the old leaven (5:7) returned to the ideas of the word of the cross and of Christ crucified (1:17). Paul wanted the Corinthians to know the full implications of that for their community purity.

At the first Passover in Egypt, the Israelites had to clean out any leaven in their houses (see Ex. 12:15, 19; 13:7; Deut. 16:34). When Paul took up that image and applied it to the "house" of the Christian fellowship (5:7), he did not make a superficial link between an aspect of the Passover and Christ's death. He understood God's redemption of Israel from Egypt as a type of His greater work of world redemption from sin through the cross.[5] Christ was the sacrificial Lamb (5:7; see Luke 22:19; 1 Pet. 1:13-21) who had already been sacrificed. But in the Jewish Passover celebration, the leaven was to be cleaned out from the house before the sacrifice. Therefore, Paul could say that the Corinthians were already "unleavened," because their Passover had already been sacrificed. God Himself had cleansed out the leaven from the community by means of Christ's sacrifice. How contradictory for the community knowingly to put some leaven back in!

Paul likened the entire Christian life to a Passover feast (5:8). The symbol of leaven and unleavened bread was made specific to the Corinthians' situation. "Malice and wickedness" related to the leaven that had entered the community through their acceptance of sin. They were arrogant against each other over allowing sin. "Sincerity and truth" in this context spoke of allowing the indwelling Christ to shine through them rather than an insincere facade of evil. That had to be done according to God's "truth" in Christ.

JUDGMENT: IN AND OUT OF THE CHURCH (5:9-13)

Paul next mentioned a previous letter he had written concerning immoral people. That shows that even before he heard about the particular problem mentioned in 5:1-8, he knew about the Corinthians' willingness to associate with immoral people. In fact, his second visit had been concerned with the problem of immorality in the church (2 Cor. 13:2).

The catalogue of virtues and vices (5:10) was for emphasis but also came very close to a point-for-point description of the Corinthians' problems.[6] The Corinthians thought Paul had told them to avoid all association with immoral people in or out of the church. They then concluded that that was impos-

---

5. On the subject of Bible-wide themes of redemption, see Graeme Goldsworthy, *Gospel and Kingdom* (Minneapolis: Winston Press, 1981).
6. See Conzelmann, *1 Corinthians,* p. 101, note 69, for other vice and virtue lists in the New Testament.

sible. But instead of seeking clarification from Paul, they went to the extreme of arguing that immorality within or without the church could be acceptable.

In that light, Paul clarified (5:11) the intention of his previous letter. When it came to an immoral brother, they should not "associate" or "eat with" such a one. Interestingly, the short list in 5:11 mentioned problems that Paul would address throughout this letter: immoral person (5); covetous (6); idolater (8-10); drunkard (11); and swindler (6). Would the Corinthians see the implications of those words to the other areas of their lives?

In 5:12-13, Paul discussed judging in and out of the church. Christian judgment was limited to those within the church. Verse 13 shows that God would judge "outside"; therefore, the sinning brother was to be cast outside, where he would be dealt with by God.

In verse 13, Paul alluded to a phrase found throughout Deuteronomy (17:7, 12; 22:24). The Deuteronomy context was that of the wilderness wanderings and settlement in Israel. That added to the already impressive list of Paul's use of Old Testament Israelite concepts in relation to the church of Jesus Christ. Paul's entire thrust of the cross (1:17) was cast into the Passover sacrifice image (5:8). Further exodus imagery will be seen in chapter 10.

USE OF UNBELIEVERS (6:1-11)

DARE TO GO TO THE UNRIGHTEOUS? SEVEN QUESTIONS (6:1-6)

The theme of judging continued from chapter 5 by Paul's use of the concepts of unrighteous versus saints and of inside versus outside. Here Paul applied the doctrines of last things and of Christ to the Corinthian problem of going to law before unbelievers. But note his question-and-answer approach. He made his initial point by asking seven straightforward questions.

Paul's emphasis in 5:1-8 was *judge* yourselves. In 5:9-13, it was judge *yourselves*. Chapter 6 elaborated on that emphasis.

In chapter 5, the Corinthians exercised no judgment upon sin. In chapter 6, the Corinthians were full of self-righteous assertions of the legal sins against them in the civil courts. Unbothered by spiritual impurity in the church, they were enraged by civil violations of their personal rights.

Question one: Did they dare to go to the unrighteous (6:1)? In light of 5:12-13, did they dare go outside for judgment? The question of judging outsiders (chap. 5) now turned to the Corinthians' allowing themselves to be judged by outsiders. Those outside the church were in the realm of God's judgment (5:13). They were the unrighteous and foolish people described by Paul in chapters 1 and 2. We might think Paul was asking how the Corinthians ever expected to find proper judgment from those kinds of people. But that would miss Paul's point. He was not arguing that pagan judges could not render just judgments.

The question related to a deeper issue, an issue brought out by the questions that follow. It related to the self-identity of the believer in the light of his future, not to the abilities and relative merits of unbelieving judges.

Questions two and three: World judgment (6:2). Paul argued from the greater (the world) to the lesser (small law courts). Perhaps we did not know that saints would judge the world (Ps. 49:14; Dan. 7:22; Matt. 19:28; Luke 22:30; Rev. 2:26; 3:21; 20:4). But Paul's point here was not to expand or support that statement. Rather, he simply meant to assert its truth in order to use its implications for the problem at hand.

If they were destined to judge the world, the cosmic perspective, why were they not able to handle small problems here and now? The answer to that question was given in verse 8. They could not handle their problems because they were acting like unbelievers.

Question four: Did they know they would judge angels (supernature) and the things of this nature (6:3)? This was the same kind of argument as in 6:2. (On judging angels, see Isa.

24:21; 2 Pet. 2:4; Jude 6; Rev. 20:10.) This again is an argument from major to minor.[7]

Question five: Should they not select judges on the basis of their account in the church (6:4)? That showed the Corinthians' misunderstanding of what made someone weak or strong. The Greek word for "no importance" is found in 1:28 and 16:11.

Question six: Was there no Christian wise enough (6:5)? The first part of this verse regarding their shame is the only nonquestion in 6:1-8 and shows the direction of Paul's answers to his questions. How ironic that those who thought themselves so wise were so foolish in the sight of God.

Question seven: Would brothers fight before unbelievers (6:6)? Paul got to the heart of the problem. On the surface, we might think that Paul had witness to unbelievers in mind, but his thoughts were in another direction, as the next verses show. The real problem was that the Corinthians were denying their true nature as children of the kingdom and were acting like those who were excluded from it.

ALREADY A DEFEAT: YOU WRONG (6:7-8)

They might have won in court, but actually they were defeated before they began. The very fact that they had lawsuits was a defeat. In light of their alignment with pagan ways, they should have let the case drop (see Matt. 5:38-42 and 1 Pet. 2:23).

Answer the questions of 6:7 for yourself, but remember the options: to act like a child of God or like a child of unrighteousness. "Defraud" came from an old verb for "to rob." Note the reversal of the terms of 6:7 in 6:8—being wronged and doing the wrong.

---

7. See Theodor H. Gaster, *The Dead Sea Scriptures* (Garden City, N.Y.: Anchor, 1976), p. 320, for the view of the elect judging angels.

UNRIGHTEOUSNESS AND THE KINGDOM (6:9-11)

Another piercing question supported Paul's perspective. Had they not understood that their fighting placed them into the camp of those excluded from the kingdom? Paul was speaking of the kingdom all along (see 4:20; 6:10; 15:24, 50; and the idea of reign, 4:8; 15:25) and just mentioned the Corinthians' future reign (6:2-3). But they were being deceived by their own ambitions (6:9; see also 15:33).

Compare 6:9-10 with 5:10-11. The Corinthians were confused about community purity, and that had spilled over into confusion about social purity. To correct that, Paul asked them to consider their true state in Christ (6:11).

He did that by supplying three contrasts to show what changes had occurred in their lives; "but . . . but . . . but . . ." (6:11). What a tremendous contrast to their past lives! The death of Christ and the presence of the Spirit had cleansed them, but was that past cleansing still evident in their daily lives? Paul clearly showed their problem. They were totally changed as children of God, but they were still allowing themselves to live in their past ways.

RELATION OF THE BODY TO THE TRINITY AND IMMORALITY (6:12-20)

THESIS REGARDING HARMONY (6:12)

Paul first supplied his thesis statement, "All things are lawful." The following verses offer elaboration and support. The focus on immorality was at the head of the list in 6:9 and comprehended all the lesser evils in the list of 6:9-11, from idolatry on down.

How are we to take this thesis statement? It is best to see it as applying to areas of life not specifically addressed in Scripture. However, in abstract the slogan was canceling freedom (12b). Though the Corinthians had a formal right to do anything, they were ending up by being mastered by evil. Paul had already said that all belonged to them (3:21-23). But ultimately all belonged to God, not the individual Corinthian. That slogan of freedom spanned the topics from 1 Corinthians

5-14 concerning the Corinthian problems with the flesh. Paul then personalized it to the situation at hand. (Because of its repetition in 10:23, it might have been a Corinthian slogan that they used to justify their immorality.) The core of profitability was mastery of self.

Paul immediately got to the point—"not all things are profitable." The Greek word for "profitable" is also used in 10:23 and 12:7, and a related form is used in 7:35 and 10:33. Paul would later make the abstract concrete by speaking of edification (10:23). But he would not do that by substituting a new legalism for their license. The way out was in a new direction.

RELATION OF THE BODY TO THE RESURRECTION AND CHRIST (6:13-20)

Paul made a general statement in 6:13. Freedom in matters of food did not equal freedom for immorality. Stomach and food were temporal, but the body was for the resurrected (6:14) Lord.

In 6:13*b*-14, Paul spoke of the resurrection patterns of eternal existence. The Corinthians had their special problems with resurrection, as chapter 15 will show. Here, Paul met them on their own ground, the implications of their antiresurrection speculation. The body was to be seen as an eternal aspect of the self, not as unimportant, temporary baggage with which they could do anything.

The body would be resurrected (6:14); therefore, the Corinthians needed their estimation of the worth of the body increased. Paul did that by reminding them of the eternal worth of their bodies, especially as focused on the Lord's own resurrection. Why would God resurrect the body, Christ's or the believer's, if it were unimportant? Because the body was an integral part of God's salvation; the spirit and the body were saved together.

The Corinthian tendency to downgrade the worth of the body was behind what seems to be, at first glance, three some what separate issues (5:1—6:20): a sinning brother (5:1-13); lawsuits (6:1-11); and sexual relationships with a prostitute (6:12-20). But the unifying thread was immorality based on a "freedom" to let the body have its own way. What the Corinthians condoned in public they also nurtured in private. Therefore, they were led into the immorality of lawsuits with Christians, and even into immorality with prostitutes. Their misunderstanding of Paul's admonishment to avoid immoral people (5:9-13) was twisted in such a way as to allow them to associate with all forms of immorality under the guise of Christian freedom.

Verse 15 draws a salvation parallel between the bodies of Christ and the Christian. The statement regarding unity with a prostitute stressed ethical incompatibility and showed what the Corinthians had forgotten, the implications of their bodies in relation to Christ's.[8] Evidently, the Corinthians did not realize that immorality had a real effect on the Christian. They thought that because the body would pass away, there was no harm done. In order to refute that, Paul quoted Genesis 2:24 (6:16).[9]

The quotation of Genesis 2:24 was aimed at proving that a real unity was made in sexual relationships. The questions of 6:15-16 were not regarding physical possibility but ethical incompatibility. By presenting his illustration of unity, Paul tried to convey clearly the absolute contradiction involved. The mild adversative ("but") heightened the contrast by noting the even more thorough-going unity of a believer with Christ (6:17). If physical union created a real unity, how much more intimate was the bond created by spiritual union with the resurrected Lord?

Paul applied the Genesis passage, which originally had the pure and serene setting of Eden, to a Corinthian and his prostitute. The quotation served to illustrate why a man was one flesh with a prostitute. The unity achieved by that immoral union was greater than the Corinthians believed. In God's

8. There was no cultic prostitution at the temple of Aphrodite during Paul's day. That was only a part of the old Greek city destroyed in 146 B.C. See Conzelmann, *1 Corinthians*, p. 12.
9. Barrett, *A Commentary on the First Epistle to the Corinthians*, pp. 66-70.

judgment, that act was a union appropriate only within the marriage bond.[10]

With verse 17, Paul drove to the heart of the matter. Intimacy with the Lord went beyond the flesh. It pierced down to the spirit. That revealed an inherent presupposition not understood by the Corinthians. Their life in Christ brought a comprehensive union of body and spirit, not a compartmentalized existence where the spirit was the Lord's, but the body could be allowed to participate in sin. Spiritual union was the basis for the Body of Christ concept, a concept not well-discerned in Corinth (see 11:27-29).

In 6:18-20, Paul gave his exhortation for action in light of what he had just developed. Immorality was a sin against the body, and the body was the temple of the Spirit, bought with a price.

The body was God's (6:19-20), not the Corinthians' possession. It was bought (6:20) with a price, the costly life of Christ. The word "therefore" has a sense of immediacy—therefore, do it now. With that sense of urgency, Paul moved to the ultimate purpose of the body. The Corinthians were to manifest the person of God, not their own lusts.

CONCLUSION

Notice the argument Paul used to move the Corinthians away from their problems with immorality and fighting. He did not substitute another legalism. Rather, he illuminated who they were in God's great redemption, and then drew out implications of that for their problems. These first six chapters were Paul's perspective for answering the following questions from the Corinthians. Not unexpectedly, their first question will concern immorality (7:1-2).

---

10. See Matt. 19:6 and Mark 10:8 for Gen. 2:24; also Eph. 5:31 regarding Christ and the church. The bride metaphor was behind much of Paul's thought, and his exposition highlighted one implication of that figure.

5

SEX AND MARRIAGE: STAYING OR CHANGING

(7:1-40)

INTRODUCTION

MARRIAGE RELATIONSHIPS

The problem.

It is good for a man not to touch a woman. (7:1)

Stop depriving one another, except by agreement for a time that you may devote yourselves to prayer, and come together again lest Satan tempt you because of your lack of self-control. (7:5)

The solution.

But because of immoralities, let each man have his own wife, and let each woman have her own husband. (7:2)

Only, as the Lord has assigned to each one, as God has called each, in this manner let him walk. And thus I direct in all the churches. (7:17)

But I say to the unmarried and to widows that it is good for them if they remain even as I. (7:8)

I think then that this is good in view of the present distress, that it is good for a man to remain as he is. (7:26)

The purpose.

But I want you to be free from concern. One who is unmarried is concerned about the things of the Lord, how he may please the

> Lord; but one who is married is concerned about the things of the world, how he may please his wife, and his interests are divided. . . . And this I say for your own benefit; not to put a restraint upon you, but to promote what is seemly, and to secure undistracted devotion to the Lord. (7:32*a*, 35)

This chapter introduces the "now concerning" phrases that are found throughout the letter from this point on (7:1, 25; 8:1; 12:1; 16:1; see also 16:12). In 7:1, the phrase introduces "the things about which you wrote." Paul began to answer some particular Corinthian questions. In that light, the other "now concerning" phrases may also introduce questions from Corinth.

Chapters 5-6 centered on fleeing immorality. Chapter 7 applied the Corinthians' calling and gifts to their misinformed desire for a false status and holiness concerning sexual relationships within marriage.

The backdrop for Paul's thoughts was a passing away world (7:31), the present distress (7:26), and the resulting shortening of time (7:29). Clearly, in Paul's mind, the end of the world was related to solving the Corinthian problem with marriage. Paul also had the doctrine of salvation on his mind (7:16). He focused them on God's gifts (7:7) and their calling (7:20, 24).

Note the use of "good" several times in this section (7:1, 8, 26, 37-38 ["well," "better"], 40 ["happier"]). Also note his careful distinctions between opinion and command (7:6, 10, 12, 25, 40).

THE PLACE FOR SEXUAL ABSTINENCE (7:1-7)

Verse 1 states Paul's general principle. He first applied the principle to marriage (7:1-7). Abstinence was good, but not required. If there was a desire for marriage, it ought to be met. Paul did not write that unopinionated, but he refrained from stating his own opinion until verses 7 and 29-35.

Verse 2 shows us the main problem, which was sexual. How should the married Christian man or woman understand the place of sexual relationships in the process of sanctification?

The first step was admitting that immoralities were all too tempting (see 5:1, 9; 6:13, 15, 18), and that only within the marriage bond could sexual relationships avoid sin.

Verse 3 expresses the duty each spouse owed to the other in order to avoid Satan's temptations (7:5). In the marriage relationship, duty took precedence over the other interests noted in 7:5. Were some not doing their duty? Verse 5 clearly shows that some, indeed, had fallen prey to a false view of the sexual union within marriage and had argued for a type of asceticism between spouses.

Verse 4 gives the reason for that balanced duty. Those who came to believe that sexual relationships in marriage were impure started depriving their spouses of sexual gratification. They withheld themselves under the guise of Christian purity. Paul responded that it was, indeed, good not to touch a woman, but that goodness had to be defined in the light of several other important conditions.

One such condition was authority. Who was the boss when it came to sexual relations in marriage? Neither the husband nor the wife. Each was under the others' authority. Why? To avoid immorality, the very subject Paul had been dealing with since chapter 5. In 6:12, the assertion of freedom had led some into sin. In 7:1-5, a false use of authority had led to sexual stresses and temptations that could also lead to sin, as 7:5 shows.

The problem clearly surfaces in verse 5. Paul told them to "stop depriving one another." They were already doing it. The word for depriving is used here and in 6:7-8 ("defraud"). They defrauded their brothers in the law courts and their wives at home. The same Greek word was used in Exodus 21:10 (in the Greek Old Testament) regarding marriage rights.

But behind that superficial, noble attempt at purity was satanic temptation to immorality. To what did "this" (7:6) refer? It appears to have referred to temporary abstinence, or possibly the entire subject of having to be married (the next three verses support the focus on having to be married). However, the idea of concession is best mirrored in the "except" of 7:5, the only concessional idea in 7:1-5. But Paul's point, whether concerning marriage or abstinence within marriage, was that it was not a command carrying God's authority. Paul never commanded marriage or abstinence for all. The next verse substantiates that.

"As I myself" (7:7) is often taken to mean unmarried. Actually, it referred to Paul's sexual control over himself, which led in turn to his being able to remain single. Paul spoke of each one's having a "gift" (see 12:4-11), the direction and ability in life given by God. This passage teaches that sexual control, not marriage, is a spiritual gift. Paul noted that sexual abstinence was good but should always be seen in relationship to the gifts God had given, not in the light of pressures to conform to human standards of status or purity.

Unmarried and Widows: Good (7:8-9)

This chapter began with the question of what was *good.* In verse 8, Paul continued his discussion of the good—this time in relation to beginning, continuing, or discontinuing the marital state. But the question was not so much marriage itself as it was the notion of whether marriage made one pure or impure. Verses 8-16 specifically relate to true and false purity in marriage.

Verse 9 has the same relationship to verse 8 as verse 2 has to verse 1: X is good (7:1, 8), but watch out for Y (7:2, 9). The issue was self-control. Here we discover that the essence of "even as I" (7:7-8) was "self-control." But the remark about not having self-control was not disparaging. It must be read in light of 7:7, where Paul clearly identified both single and married states as gifts from God. Therefore, "self-control" has to be seen in the specific sense of being able to live a single life as a God-given call. For those whom God had not gifted in that manner, sexual abstinence was optional and temporary at best.

Marriage, Divorce, and Sanctification (7:10-16)

In verses 10-11, Paul took up the question of whether those already married should stay wed. Paul next discussed marriage of a believer with an unbeliever in 7:12-16. He stressed consideration for the unbeliever's attitude and assumed the believer would be of a mind to keep the marriage intact (vv. 12-13).

In 7:14, Paul uncovered the fear that caused some to send away the unbelieving partners. They thought that marriage to an unbeliever hindered the process of sanctification. Paul countered that mistaken notion by saying that actually the reverse was true: They did not make the Christian impure; rather, the Christian made them pure. Husband and children benefited from the believer's godliness.

But how could an unbeliever be sanctified? The answer hinges on understanding the source of this particular sanctification. We are used to thinking of sanctification as beginning in God (e.g., 6:11). That use of sanctification meant full redemption and cleansing. But the word itself simply meant that something was set apart, usually for a holy purpose. Thus, what gave the word its power in 6:11 was the following phrase, "in the name of the Lord."

The same is true in 7:14. The "setting apart" was conditioned by the medium: "through" the husband or wife. That was not redemptive sanctification originating in God. It was the practical exposure to holy things of God by exposure to the believing spouse. The believer was not defiled. He or she could actually have a sanctifying impact on spouse and children. The believer could, to that extent, set the family apart in the sphere of Christian influence. No wonder Paul said the believer should not separate from the unbeliever.

But what if the unbeliever wanted to divorce (7:15-16)? That partner should be allowed to go. Though the unbeliever would thus be denied the possible sanctification offered by the believing spouse, Paul clearly disavowed any coercion from the Christian partner.

The believer was not bound in that case. But not bound to what? Is divorce in view, or simply one's attempts to keep the mate from departing? I do not see any ultimate difference between those two options. The issue was the dissolution of the marriage. For the unbeliever to depart meant divorce. But the point of this entire chapter was to help the Corinthians relax and have peace in remaining in their present states, not seeking something else. Here, the point was "peace," specifically over the matter of having to let a marriage end in divorce. The believer had to remember God's call to peace. That call was certain and ongoing and brought to bear the Old Testament concept of *shalom* (peace).

In light of the sanctifying influence of the believing spouse, naturally the desire to save the unbeliever would arise and be very strong, with eternity in view. It is to that strong desire that Paul addressed the words of 7:16. Will you save the mate? The believer could not honestly know.[1] Therefore, Paul concluded that the matter should be left in God's hands. Any coercive moves from the believer to keep the unbeliever would be an intrusion into the sphere of God's sovereignty and a disruption of His intended call to peace.

THESIS: STAY WHERE YOU WERE CALLED (7:17-24)

This section is the watershed between the discussions of immorality (7:1-16) and of devotion to the Lord in the end-times (7:25-40). Paul encouraged the Corinthians to stay with God's calling (7:17-24).

Verses 17-24 show Paul's guiding principle and the outworking of "called us to peace" (7:15). The Corinthians were not to seek a supposedly better spiritual standing by changing their marital, social, or religious status. We see this in verses 17, 20, and 24, which frame this little paragraph on calling.

Verse 17 states the principle once: walk as called. The stress was on who did the calling ("as the Lord has assigned" and "as God has called each"). To make the changes of which Paul spoke was to go contrary to what the Lord and the Father had found acceptable. If one's position was proper enough to be the environment for God's calling, why would one feel com-

---

1. Sakae Kubo, "I Corinthians VII.16: Optimistic or Pessimistic?" *New Testament Studies* 24, pp. 539-44.

pelled to change it? The next verses uncover the sinister motives behind such alterations.

Verses 18-19 elaborate religious alterations that related to the Jew and the Greek. Evidently there was pressure to conform to old religious ways in order to gain prestige, a common failing of the Corinthians. Verse 19 gives the reason for not making that kind of change. It was of no account with God. That was also true of marriage. Those alterations and the need to say what Paul did in verse 17 were part of why there was a question about whether it was good to touch a woman. It is also possible that the factions spoken of in chapter 1 revolved around the answers to those assertions of purity.

Paul stated the principle a second time (7:20). There should not be any societal alterations (7:21). That change was motivated by worry over one's social status. But Paul replied that all were equal. The center of Paul's thoughts on remaining where one was called is in verse 22. "In the Lord" was to be the gauge for one's status, making the slaves free and the free slaves. All were to be directed His way; therefore, all were placed on the same level before Him. No religious or societal changes could improve one's standing with the Lord.

Verse 23 asserts a key truth: the Corinthians were to understand that they were serving God, not man, whether they were slaves or free. They not only missed that in this case, but also in chapter 3 regarding leaders.

Paul stated the principle a third time (7:24). The issue was remaining with God and not departing from Him to join the ranks of slaves to human criteria for status.

VIRGINS (7:25-38)

SPARING TROUBLE (7:25-28)

Paul now turned his attention to marriage and virgins. He first mentioned historical concerns (7:25-26). The translation "present distress" (7:26) should be changed to "the present constraint." Paul's mind was on constraints that came to the married, not political or social upheavals. The same Greek word is translated "constraint" in 7:37 and "compulsion" in 9:16. He specifically defined the nature of the "present" in 7:28-29, 31.

In 2 Corinthians 6:4 and 12:10, two lists of Paul's afflictions, "constraint" took on the sense of "distress." But when the word was used apart from an explicit list of persecutions, it meant "compulsion" or "constraint" (1 Cor. 9:16; 2 Cor. 9:7; Philem. 14). I see no reason to break that pattern here. Therefore, the translation "the present constraint" is better than "distress."[2] The main constraint Paul had in mind was that being married cut into one's time to serve the Lord (7:32-35). But Paul's primary point was that "a man" should "remain as he is" (7:26). That was not a repeat of Paul's commands in 7:17, 20, and 24. Rather, it referred to the condition of being single and wondering what to do about getting married (to one of the *virgins* mentioned in 7:25).

Throughout this section, Paul addressed the question of virgins' marrying or remaining single by speaking to single men (probably potential fiances, 7:26-34*a*) and the fathers of single women (7:36-38). Those were the ones responsible for making the final decision of marriage. But why did Paul spend so much time on that subject? Because it allowed him to develop his view that even marriage must be evaluated with reference to how it fostered devotion to the Lord (7:35). The Corinthians were rightly worried about sin and wrongly worried about status. Paul wanted them to focus on the central issue, undistracted devotion to the Lord.

We can see from verse 27 how careful Paul was not to cause a knee-jerk reaction to his teaching. Throughout this chapter, Paul gave his own preferences concerning marriage and the single state. But he did not want the Corinthians to respond to his teaching as they had responded to that of others—by thoughtless conformity in order to gain status. He simply wanted them to be informed regarding the nature of their calling and the times.

2. F. W. Grosheide, *Commentary on the First Epistle to the Corinthians* (Grand Rapids: Eerdmans, 1953), p. 175.

The first question and answer of verse 27 balanced Paul's affirmation of the single life in verse 26. Divorce ("to be released") was out of the question. That is, being married was a sacred and sanctifying state (7:10-11, 14). The second question and answer returned to the argument for the better state of singleness. A single person should not feel under a divine command to "seek a wife." Verse 28 supports that. Sin was not the question—being spared trouble in the flesh was. "Trouble in this life" is defined by verses 29-35.

THE SHORTENED TIME (7:29-31)

Due to little time (7:29), Paul wanted to help them minimize the *diversions* and *concern* of life. The goal of that was "undistracted devotion to the Lord" (7:35). That expectation of the future return of Christ sounds the beginning (1:7) and end (16:22*b*) notes of this letter. The backdrop for Paul's thoughts here was a passing-away world (7:29-31). This section concerned the effect of the world (7:32-34) on Christian devotion. Paul wanted them to see the true nature of the time so that temporary functions would not blur eternal priorities (see 6:12). They were to hold all worldly concerns with an open hand.

UNDISTRACTED DEVOTION TO THE LORD (7:32-35)

The goal of Paul's views on marriage and the single life is in verse 35. Paul's thoughts echoed the words of Christ (see Matt. 6:25, 27-28, 31, 34). The idea was not to be free from all concern. That could not happen even for the single person. The goal was to have as singular a life of devotion to the Lord as was possible within God's gifting of the individual.

Without verse 35, Paul's statements in verses 32-34 could have been easily misunderstood. But verse 35 supplies the reason for this entire section. In 6:12, the verb form of "benefit" (7:35) was translated "profitable." Though the Corinthians were free to marry, Paul argued that the most profitable way (in the sense of time devoted to the Lord) was the single life. Paul's thoughts reflect the outworking of his philosophy of the glorification of God (see 6:20). The glory of God was applied to each area of life. When it came to marriage, Paul had asked how one could best glorify God. Two facts of life determined his answer: (1) the end of the world was near; and (2) the single life minimized the distractions of that passing-away world.

On that basis, and working only within the limits of God's gift (7:7), Paul argued that the single life could best glorify God on earth. That shows that Paul was thinking of quantity, not quality. The single person could have more time for service to the Lord. What a great perspective for the nobility and effectiveness of the God-gifted single life.

Paul desired all to be settled down and focused on the Lord. The idea was like the Mary and Martha incident in Luke 10:38-42. Mary was settled down at the feet of Jesus, while Martha was busy with many things. In fact, the word for "distracted" (Luke 10:40) comes from the same Greek root as did Paul's "undistracted" in 7:35. Paul and Jesus also used the same Greek word for "worried" and "concerned."

VIRGINS GIVEN OR KEPT: NO SIN (7:36-38)

This section answers the question of fathers concerning whether they should marry off their virgins.[3] Paul left the choice of what would be "seemly" (7:35) in their own situations up to them (7:36). The teaching of 7:9 was addressed to the unmarried and would, therefore, relate here.

If the girl was "of full age, and if it must be so," she should be allowed to marry. Clearly, even with the cultural authority of the father over his daughter, the nature and desires of the daughter were considered.

To stress the potential problem again, Paul said that sin was not the issue (7:36, and twice in 7:28). For Martha of Jesus' day or the married Corinthian of Paul's day, there was no sin in being distracted with the affairs of life. But for Mary and the

3. See Grosheide, *Commentary on the First Epistle to the Corinthians,* p. 182, for arguments against "any man" being a reference to fiancés.

single in Corinth, both Paul and Jesus could only describe their focused devotion as better.

Paul then introduced the concept of better (7:37-38). "Better" has to be defined by the previous context. Due to the nature of the times as shortened, and given one's ability to control sexual desires, the single life was better than married life because it allowed more time for serving the Lord.

WIDOWS AND REMARRIAGE (7:39-40)

Upon the death of their husbands, widows were free to remarry. But they were to only marry "in the Lord" (7:39), most likely meaning "to a Christian." Once again, Paul encouraged his readers to define life and happiness his way. Why would the widow be happier if she remained single? Because of the developed definition of "good" and "better" in the preceding verses. Single, she would have more time for the Lord.

SUMMARY

Throughout this chapter, Paul dealt with the general problem of the appropriateness of marriage and of sexual relationships within marriage. Perhaps the Corinthians' questions were something like "Is sex unclean?" and "Is it bad to be married?" Against their false views of purity, Paul developed the implications of God's individual calling. He hoped some would see the special benefit of the single life. That life would be the sign of a gift of God (7:7), but above all it would allow for "undistracted devotion to the Lord" (7:35).

6

CONCERNING IDOLS
AND THEIR SACRIFICES

(8:1—11:1)

INTRODUCTION

The problem.

Now concerning things sacrificed to idols, we know that we all
have knowledge. Knowledge makes arrogant, but love edifies.
(8:1)

For through your knowledge he who is weak is ruined, the
brother for whose sake Christ died. (8:11)

The solution.

But food will not commend us to God; we are neither the worse if
we do not eat, nor the better if we do eat. But take care lest this
liberty of yours somehow become a stumbling block to the weak.
(8:8-9)

Therefore, if food causes my brother to stumble, I will never eat
meat again, that I might not cause my brother to stumble. (8:13)

The purpose.

What do I mean then? That a thing sacrificed to idols is anything,
or that an idol is anything? No, but I say that the things which the
Gentiles sacrifice, they sacrifice to demons, and not to God; and
I do not want you to become sharers in demons. (10:19-20)

Whether, then, you eat or drink or whatever you do, do all to the
glory of God. Give no offense either to Jews or to Greeks or to

the church of God; just as I also please all men in all things, not
seeking my own profit, but the profit of the many, that they may
be saved. (10:31-33)

The large section of 8:1—11:1 concerned food that had been
sacrificed to idols in one of Corinth's many temples and then
sold in the local stores. Could a Christian eat that food? The
Corinthians' answers to that question created problems that
evoked several contrasts from Paul.

The first contrast was between the potentially opposing effects of knowledge and love (8:1). That related to a second contrast between arrogance and edification—two concepts echoed
throughout the letter, especially in chapters 12-14. A final contrast was between knowing some*thing* or loving God (8:2-3).
That contrast formed both the rebuke and the solution to the
Corinthians' problem. The real issue was love for God resulting in love for His children (e.g., 9:19). The specific issue of
idol-sacrificed meats was simply the vehicle for teaching that
timeless truth.

The focus of the entire argument of chapters 8-10 centered
on the problem of and solution to liberty's causing one to
stumble. The Greek word translated "liberty" in 8:9 occurs
again in 9:4-6, 12, and 18 and was linked in sense to "free"
(9:1) and "profitable" (10:23).

Paul used the specific example of meats sacrificed to idols to
show the Corinthians how their freedom was misused and was
resulting in ruining a brother (8:11). Then, in chapter 9, he
would compare himself to the freedom-edification problem by
the example of his nonuse of payment for his ministry. Finally,
in chapter 10, he would use the illustration of ancient Israel to
show that membership in God's redeemed community was no
automatic guard against avoiding His displeasure. The
Israelites had fallen into idolatry in the wilderness and had suf-
fered the consequences.

But what had that last point about Israel's idolatry to do
with the Corinthians? The answer is found at the end of
chapter 10, where Paul returned again to the issue of idol meats

that began chapter 8. But in chapter 10, Paul uncovered the real and potentially disqualifying truth behind the exercise of the Corinthians' freedom: they were participating with demons.

INTRODUCTION: KNOWLEDGE (8:1-3)

In verses 1-3, Paul gave an orientation to the basic issue. In 7:1 and 7:25, the statement after the "now concerning" phrase was the essence of Paul's answer. The same was true in 8:1. The question may have come from those who thought eating idol meats was wrong: "Isn't it wrong to eat that meat?" Or the ones who wanted to eat idol meat may have urged Paul to tell the squeamish they did not know the truth about meats. Actually, both groups were being addressed by Paul, the weak in conscience and the ones who asserted their knowledge. Therefore, Paul's statement in 8:1*b* was a direct answer to both groups' questions and needs.

Why would he say "we know that we all have knowledge" (8:1)? Evidently some in Corinth had a you-should-know-better attitude toward those who could not eat meat with a good conscience. The problem was not what people knew, but how they acted upon that knowledge. Knowledge was defined in 8:1*b*-2. It made people puffed up and was not an end in itself. That last point was the key. Paul was not arguing against knowledge but against knowledge applied without love—the pervasive Corinthian problem. With one fell swoop, Paul showed the irrelevance of knowledge for the problem at hand. Knowledge made "arrogant;" love edified. Arrogance and love—the two poles between which hung most of the Corinthian problems.

Paul gave his thesis in 8:1*b*. Arrogance was related to knowledge as love was related to edification. Knowledge and pride had combined in Corinth to produce a false freedom resulting in sexual (chaps. 5-7) and worship problems (chaps. 8-14). Paul tried to correct those problems by focusing on edifying love.

Paul then gave two examples, one of knowledge and one of

love (8:2-3). The situation described was of someone who had come to a convinced and settled assertion of knowing something; in this case, knowing there was nothing wrong with idol meats for dinner. But the issue was not knowledge. It was about *how* one knew something ("known *as* he ought to know"). The person described had gained knowledge but had stopped before he had also gained love. Next, Paul showed the ultimate object of love and the goal of knowledge (8:3). The object of love was God. The goal of knowledge was being known by Him.

Those truths must have brought two surprises to the readers: (1) that knowing the truth about the issue was not enough— love was needed; and (2) that love was not primarily focused on fellow human beings but on God. Those thoughts may surprise us as well if we tend to focus more on how to solve a problem than on human and divine love. The concept of loving God alluded back to the quotation in 2:9, "for those who love Him," and the whole discussion of wisdom. Loving God also related to correcting the problem of commendation in 8:8 and the perspective of 8:11-12.

The Effect of Knowledge Without Love (8:4-13)

ONLY ONE GOD (8:4-6)

In 8:4-6, Paul listed some of the things that everyone knew about (8:1). His first point concerned the nonreality of idols—that is, the fact that the god represented by any idol did not really exist (8:4). Paul's second point asserted the uniqueness of the one true God (8:5-6).

That exposed the core of the problem with eating idol meats. Those people were not vegetarians. They were concerned that they might be participating in something that concerned other gods and lords. That was what offended their conscience before the Lord. In verse 5, Paul appears to contradict himself and assert that there were many gods and lords. But his point was this: Though the god specifically represented by an idol did not really exist, there were unseen beings behind the idol. Paul would make that explicit in chapter 10.

The point made in verse 5, however, was just the first part of the for-yet statement completed in verse 6. The key was the phrase "for us." Others were involved with hidden spirits behind the idols, but, for the Christian, basic knowledge asserted only one God.

God was described (8:6) in such a way as to exclude all other beings from the realm of potency. Note the use of "from whom," "for Him," "through whom," and "through Him." The sole supremacy of God must be considered when Paul again discusses idols in chapter 10 and in 12:1-3.

God was the Father, the source of all, and the only reason for our existence ("we exist for Him," 4:6). Then the Lord was described as the vehicle of creation and our existence. To some, there were many gods and lords, all beckoning for service. But for the Christian, only one God could demand total service, and only one Lord had made that service possible.

KNOWLEDGE UNTO EDIFICATION (8:7-13)

Paul's thesis was that knowledge made arrogant, but love edified (8:1). He had spent the first six verses delineating the knowledge that could make arrogant. Though it contained the great truths of God's sovereignty, not all were aware of it (8:7). Paul had given the position of the "knowing" in 8:1-6. In 8:7-13, Paul outlined how the arrogance of such knowledge could be turned into the edification of love.

Arrogance could end up causing a brother to stumble (8:9-13). And that brother was placed within the context of Christ's redeeming love ("the brother for whose sake Christ died," 8:11). If Christ went so far as to die to help that brother, Paul concluded that anyone should give up idol meats to keep him from stumbling.

Some in Corinth still thought that idol evil had rubbed off on sacrificial meats (8:7). They did not have the knowledge of which Paul spoke in 8:4: "We know that there is no such thing as an idol in the world, and that there is no God but one."

When they ate those meats, their consciences were being defiled.

But how could they not have known? Had they not been taught those things? Yes, they had been told, probably several times by the stronger brothers alone. But being told was not the point—conscience was. And in this case, their sense of conscience lagged behind their knowledge. In one sense, they knew, but could not accept. Past associations still held ("accustomed to the idol until now" [8:7]).

Those believers ate food "as if it were sacrificed to an idol" (8:7); that is, as if the idol was a spiritual reality. That perception on their part caused a defiled conscience. The cause of that perception was a "weak" conscience, a concept occuring five more times in 8:9-12.

In 8:8, Paul unfolded the worries behind the idol meat problem by addressing the false assertions from the side of the "strong." They were not "the better" because they ate the meats, and the weak were not "the worse" because they did not eat. Food, eaten or uneaten, had no power of commendation before God. Note how that cut across all lines of self-effort and pierced to the inner person, to conscience.

Paul did not question the genuine "liberty" (8:9) some had to eat idol meats. He would even strengthen and elaborate that freedom in 10:29-30. But he did warn them that liberty alone could become a "stumbling block to the weak." Liberty needed love.

Those who had knowledge (8:10) wielded a great power of example. The weak person merely saw; there is no mention here of the stronger Christian's verbally trying to convince the weaker to eat in a temple. The weak person could be "strengthened" (8:10) to eat by seeing the strong.

The Greek word for "strengthened" came from the same verb translated "edifies" in 8:1. Love could edify, but so could knowledge without love—an edification that ruined "the brother for whose sake Christ died" (8:11). The exercise of knowledge without love could lead to those results, thus proving Paul's thesis from 8:1. That was yet another example of

Paul's great desire to keep from voiding the cross of Christ (1:17).

Sin against Christ was to be forever avoided (8:12-13). Who would have had the perspective of 8:12? Would the Corinthians have purposely set out to ruin their brethren? Probably not. But they had missed the perspective of 8:12, because they were caught up in the exercise of their own selfish freedom rather than caught up with carefully living out the implications of Christ's redeeming love. Paul, by contrast, was always Christ-centered. Whatever he knew about the truth of God was always used to build Christians up, not to flaunt his own private freedom. The fuller implications and illustrations of that philosophy would be drawn out in chapter 9.

When put into the above perspective, who would not conclude with Paul that meat should be forever avoided (8:13)? Only those who would persist in being free at the expense of others. And there were many of that kind in Corinth. Therefore, Paul would have to deal with several other examples of that Corinthian insistence: women's head coverings (11), the abuse of the Lord's table (11), and spiritual gifts (12-14).

WHY PAUL RESTRICTED HIMSELF FOR THE WEAK AND IGNORANT
(9:1-26)

APOSTOLIC PROOFS "TO SOME" (9:1-3)

Chapter 9 concerns Paul's defense of his apostolic rights. But how did that relate to the discussion in chapter 8? Both chapters concerned the use of a person's rights as viewed through two standards, arrogance and edification. Chapter 8 showed how love needed to be exercised regarding idol meats. Chapter 9 shows how Paul exercised love in the use of his rights as an apostle. All the thoughts initially drive toward 9:19-23. Verse 19 sums it up: "For though I am free from all men, I have made myself a slave to all, that I might win the more." Verse 22 returns the focus to that of chapter 8: "To the weak I became weak, that I might win the weak. . . ."

In 9:1, Paul asked four questions that were foundational to

establishing his full authority and freedom as an apostle. The first question concerned his freedom. "Free" was closely related to liberty (the same Greek word translated "right" in chap. 9). For Paul and the Corinthians, freedom was an outgrowth of one's knowledge. Did Paul have freedom? It all depended on his knowledge. Therefore, after his initial assertion of his freedom in 9:1 (his question assumed a yes answer), his next questions probed the ground of his freedom: his knowledge.

The second question of 9:1 asserted his commission as an apostle. None in Corinth could claim that level of authority. The third question showed his commission as coming directly from a meeting with the risen Lord.

The fourth question brought the entire subject much closer to home. Were not the Corinthians themselves a living product of Paul's work in the Lord, an affirmation of the Lord's blessing upon him? They thought very highly of themselves. To be consistent, they would have to acknowledge the same high regard for their spiritual father (2:1-5).

The next verse (9:2) elaborated that last point. The Corinthians' very existence as Christians was the sign and seal confirming Paul's apostleship. But Paul had more to say because of the "others" who doubted his apostleship and because of the Corinthians' need to understand how pervasive and important his point was. He was not simply talking about idol meats. He was talking about the foundation of all Christ-centered ministries of the gospel.

Paul's numerous mentions of being under examination reflected a pervasive problem. The Greek word for "examine" is seen in 2:14-15; twice in 4:3; 9:3; 10:25, 27; and 14:24. Such examining was, however, only the right of the spiritual person (2:15), and the Corinthians certainly did not qualify (3:1-3). But the point of this section was not to bully the Corinthians with Paul's authority; rather, it was to edify and save (9:19). So Paul humbled himself to provide the best explanation for his examiners.

THE QUESTION OF AUTHORITY (9:4-23)

Paul's method of edification was to ask eleven questions on his rights (9:4-12). Such questioning created a lively exchange of thought and served to probe the hearers and elicit the proper response from their own considerations.

Questions of freedom (9:4-6). The issue was clearly Paul's "rights" (9:4-6, 12). The Corinthians' strong views about their rights had created a widespread problem, leading Paul to deal with their views on civil (6), marital (7), and religious rights (8). They had the wrong idea of both the nature and the purpose of authority.

In 9:4-5, Paul dealt with two subjects, eating and drinking (9:4), and marriage (9:5). One aspect of the former had been dealt with in chapter 8, and the latter in chapter 7. Here the issue was simply that Paul had rights. He will later explain why he did not use them. Somewhat sarcastically, Paul asked why the Christian community was willing to bear the expense—for everyone except Paul and Barnabas (9:6).

Paul was trying to get the Corinthians to come to grips with the reason why he, unlike others, did not receive support. The answer was not that he did not have the right. The answer would go in a different direction. The expected answer to those questions was, "No, Paul, you and Barnabas do have the right to all those things." That would set them up for Paul's next step—telling why he did not use his rights.

Three parables (9:7). Paul now answered the questions he had posed in 9:4-6. He began by giving three parables from human work (9:7). To answer his three questions from the situations of soldier, farmer, and shepherd, we would have to say that no one would do those things without sharing in the rewards. Few, if any, work for free.

Two supports from what is written, and an application to the Corinthians (9:8-11). Paul then answered his questions in scriptural terms (9:8-10). As if to anticipate an objection to the seemingly human bent of his argument in 9:7, Paul countered that he was also speaking according to God's law. He offered a quotation from Deuteronomy 25:4 to prove his right to support.

In the book of Deuteronomy, the passage Paul quoted is surrounded by various laws concerning mercy and justice toward one's fellow countrymen. Deuteronomy 24 contains divorce regulations (24:1-4); military exemption for newlyweds (24:5); humanitarianism where pledges were concerned (24:10-13); wages for the poor (24:15); death penalties for fathers and sons (24:16); fairness for orphans, widows, and aliens (24:17-18); and gleaning restrictions (24:19-22). Chapter 25 discussed humaneness in punishment (25:1-3), the passage quoted by Paul (25:4), and then a section on levirite marriage (25:5-10).

As can be seen from the brief survey of the contents of Deuteronomy 24-25, the passage quoted by Paul concerning animals appears rather unexpectedly in the middle of laws concerning humane treatment of people. Unlike the other surrounding commands, that one does not have an appended reason for obedience. Also, its almost proverbial tone gives the impression of a principle rather than a strictly literal agricultural procedure.[1]

The ox was not to be muzzled; but why? The Old Testament context outlined various balances that needed to be observed. The poor needed their garments and wages (Deut. 24:10-15); each was put to death for his own sins (Deut. 24:16); the redemption from Egypt was a sign to be generous regarding a pledge and gleaning (Deut. 24:17-22); and even in punishment, personal integrity was to be respected (Deut. 25:1-3).

But what did all of that have to do with not putting a muzzle on an ox? Deuteronomy 25:4 appears to function as a proverbial and figurative summary of the preceding exhortations. The image of the ox was used as the illustrative vehicle for conveying a principle by a movement from the lesser to the greater. If a lowly ox had inalienable rights, how much more would fellow Israelites? That enabled Paul to say, "God is not concerned

---

1. C. F. Keil and F. Delitzsch, *Biblical Commentary on the Old Testament* vol. 3, ed. James Martin (Edinburgh: T. & T. Clark, 1867), pp. 421-22.

about oxen, is He?" (9:9). His question's intent is clear. Could anyone think God put that passage in His law just to care for oxen?

Many commentators apparently think that was the point of the passage. The general trend of opinion regarding this quotation is that Paul has not only openly ignored the literal meaning of the Old Testament,[2] but that he has even claimed it was never there in the first place.[3] But if one sees that Deuteronomy 25:4 itself is a principle that in its original context had a primary significance for human as well as livestock relationships, then Paul has neither violated the historical context nor indulged in extreme typology.[4]

Paul argued that God had spoken about oxen for the sake of human beings. His "altogether" was a strong way of saying that given the choice between focusing on provisions for oxen or provisions for people, the focus must be altogether on human concerns. The Greek word leaves secondary applications open (see Jer. 7:21; Ezek. 20:25; Matt. 9:13; 12:7; Heb. 6:6; 1 Pet. 1:12).

Verse 11 sums up the thrust so far. The link is clear between Paul's spiritual service and his right to material reward. Human illustrations and scriptural law proved Paul's right to support.

"Others?" (9:12). Paul returned to the unseen group of "others" (see 9:2). In 9:2, that group doubted Paul's apostleship. In 9:12, the group is best defined by 9:5: "the rest of the apostles, and the brothers of the Lord, and Cephas." The argument is again from the lesser to the greater. Surely

2. Henry St. John Thackeray, *The Relation of St. Paul to Contemporary Jewish Thought* (London: Macmillan, 1900), p. 193.
3. See also F. F. Bruce, *1 and 2 Corinthians* (London: Oliphants, 1971), p. 84, who states that Paul's "argument may clash with modern exegetical method and western sentiment, but he must be allowed to mean what he says"; and James Barr, *Old and New in Interpretation* (London: SCM, 1966), p. 109.
4. See W. C. Kaiser, Jr., "The Current Crisis in Exegesis and the Apostolic Use of Deuteronomy 25:4 in 1 Corinthians 9:8-10," *Journal of the Evangelical Theological Society* 21 (1978), pp. 3-18, and H. Cunliffe-Jones, *Deuteronomy* (London: SCM, 1951), p. 140.

Paul not only had a right to support, but even a greater right because of his special relationship to the Corinthians.

Verse 9:12*b*, however, introduces the key concept for this section: possession of rights does not demand usage of rights. Note how carefully Paul had sized up the situation in Corinth regarding support. He had done this with the gospel always in view (see 1:17), even though it made him have to "endure all things."

Paul did not want to cause any "hindrance to the gospel of Christ" (9:12). The sense of hindrance is akin to "stumbling block" (8:9) and "stumble" (8:13). Therefore, the hindrance of which Paul spoke could be to Christians and non-Christians alike.

Temple-gospel parallel (9:13-14). Why, then, did Paul offer yet another reinforcement of his rights (9:13-14) after he had just said he did not use them? Because the Corinthians thought that Paul's nonuse of rights meant he did not have them to begin with. So Paul again emphasized his freedom. Without their firm grasp of his rights, the power of his reason for not using them would be lost.

That last affirmation of Paul's rights was the most powerful. The entire gospel ministry of the glory of God in Christ was made analogous to the great priestly ministry at the Jerusalem Temple. The point was that it had always been God's way to provide for the servants of His covenants. The Lord had affirmed that in Matthew 10:10; Luke 10:7-8; and 1 Timothy 5:18.

Preaching without using full authority (9:15-18). Verse 15 returns to 9:12*b* and Paul's nonuse of his rights. The last part of 9:15 shows how strongly Paul was committed to his position. But it was not his reputation that concerned him—it was the gospel's.

"For" (9:16-18) shows the pressure that was on Paul. He had nothing to boast about in the sense of his free-will involvement in the gospel ministry. He considered himself "under compulsion" (9:16) to such a degree that to cease his ministry would bring God's "woe" upon him.[5]

Verse 17 clarifies that. Paul's ministry was a matter of entrustment, not salary, relating back to his discussion of being a steward (4:2). Paul presented two views of ministry. The first was the voluntary type, in which the minister was a free agent who, after some deliberation, decided that he could contribute his services to the ministry of the gospel. The second was the "against-my-will" type ("involuntarily" rather than "against my will" would bring out Paul's word play with "voluntarily"). That person served without choice, like a slave under the compulsion of his slave-oriented destiny. Paul was not addressing the question of liking or not liking his work. The issue was his attitude toward his involvement. Was he a free agent or a steward under compulsion?[6]

But Paul did have a reward, though not the monetary kind (9:18). His reward was to preach the gospel free of charge and thereby not use his rights (see 9:12, 15). But all of that was not an end in itself, as if Paul achieved his goal when he gave free ministry. No. Free ministry was only the means for Paul to achieve his true reward, which was saving as many people as possible.

A brief word needs to be said concerning how Paul actually did make his living. He certainly took money and goods from some churches, so what did he mean in saying he preached free of charge? We must conclude that Paul spoke of his specific actions in the area of Corinth, not of his entire ministry.[7] Let the final word come from Paul:

> Or did I commit a sin in humbling myself that you might be exalted, because I preached the gospel of God to you without

---

5. Note how that passion for ministry was so balanced and restrained in his discussion of marriage and present constraints in chapter 7.
6. Hans Conzelmann, *I Corinthians,* ed. James W. Leitch (Philadelphia: Fortress, 1975), p. 158.
7. See R. B. Hughes, "The Issue of 'Free' Ministry," in *Second Corinthians* (Chicago: Moody, 1983), pp. 103-7.

charge? I robbed other churches, taking wages from them to
serve you; and when I was present with you and was in need, I
was not a burden to anyone; for when the brethren came from
Macedonia, they fully supplied my need, and in everything I kept
myself from being a burden to you, and will continue to do so.
As the truth of Christ is in me, this boasting of mine will not be
stopped in the regions of Achaia. Why? Because I do not love
you? God knows I do! But what I am doing, I will continue to
do, that I may cut off opportunity from those who desire an opportunity to be regarded just as we are in the matter about which
they are boasting. (2 Cor. 11:7-12)

Free from all but a slave to save all (9:19-23). Paul clarified
why he gave up his rights; he wanted to win more people to
Christ (see the use of "win" and "save" in 9:19-22).

Notice the groups from which Paul drew his examples in
9:20-22. There are four, probably interrelated, groups: (1) the
Jews, (2) those under the law, (3) those without the law, and (4)
the weak. The point of Paul's conformity to those groups was
to save some (9:22).[8] Paul's desire ends both this section and
the concluding section on the subject of idolatry (10:14-33).

Paul made it clear that one's knowledge had to be used to
edify others. His being all things to all people did not destroy
his good conscience before God. He was able to avoid legalism
("not being myself under the Law" [9:20]) and license ("not
being without the law of God but under the law of Christ"
[9:21]). What appeared to be a vacillation or a weakness on
Paul's part was in reality the very exercise of his Christ-
centered and cross-furthering ministry.

In 9:19-23, Paul showed the whole scope of his ministry, of
which the Corinthians had seen but a part. They accused him
of being limited because he did not fully use apostolic rights.
That was a value judgment without the context of a person's
whole life. Paul showed that his limitations were universal and
ministry oriented.

---

8. H. Chadwick, " 'All Things to All Men' (I Cor. IX.22)," *New Testament
Studies* 1 (1954-55), pp. 261-75.

Verse 23 provides a transition out of the first major discussion of the problem of arrogant knowledge and into the discussion of how it was possible for a believer to be disqualified and undergo God's judgment.

The aim of a sharer: to be approved (9:24-26). Throughout this letter, the issue of who was approved was key. The Corinthians used all-too-human standards to judge worth. Paul continually and from several different perspectives tried to instill the divine view of what made someone approved. In verse 23, he raised the issue of being a "fellow-partaker" of the gospel. All that Paul just described was a sharing in the gospel. Where did that leave the arrogant exercises of Corinthian freedom? The clearly not-too-positive answer to that question led Paul into a long section on the possibility of the Corinthians' falling under God's displeasure.

Paul next introduced two illustrations from the world of sports. The site of the Isthmian games was only about seven miles from Corinth. The first illustration singled out a unique way of running a race—the way that won (9:24). That verse ends with a straightforward exhortation to the Corinthians. What corrections would they need to make to run to win? But, more to the point, what did Paul have in mind when he implied there was a way for them to run and lose?

Paul provided a partial answer to that question in verse 25. "Self-control" would be at the heart of the winning way to run. The contrast with an earthly wreath implies that Paul had the entrance into the heavenly state in mind when speaking of the end of the race.

Paul then applied the illustrations to himself. Had someone accused him of running without aim? Some doubted that his ways reflected those of an apostle (9:2). But apart from the probable behind-the-scenes slander, Paul's thrust was toward including himself along with any other Christian as a potential candidate for disqualification (9:27). Even the great and qualified apostle Paul had to practice what he preached.

The specific point of disqualification that had been developed in the immediate context was the act of hindering the gospel among saved and unsaved alike. To avoid that error, Paul said "we endure all things, that we may cause no hindrance to the gospel of Christ" (9:12). Did the Corinthians think they could not possibly disqualify? If they did, the next words of Paul would shatter such false security.

PAST AND PRESENT DISQUALIFICATIONS (10:1-22)

THE PAST PRIVILEGES OF ISRAEL (10:1-5)

Paul concluded chapter 9 by showing that his main goal was not the exercise of his rights but the effective striving to win men to Christ while maintaining his own personal discipline. Chapter 10 commenced an illustrative argument showing that though one had a relationship with God, he still had to keep himself from human lust and pride. That arose from Paul's remarks in 9:27 about being excluded himself due to lack of personal discipline, and from the Corinthians' tendency to participate in local idolatrous practices.

In 9:27, Paul raised the issue of his personal disqualification should he ever lack "self-control" or not "buffet" his body. But how could he or any Christian be disqualified, and what could that mean specifically? Chapter 10 gives particular examples of the idolatry that caused the Israel of old to be disqualified, and of what could cause the same for the Corinthians. By showing that, Paul exposed a shocking truth. The Corinthians, for all their supposed exercise of religious freedom, were actually involved with idolatry.

No wonder Paul could not yet speak to the Corinthians as spiritual people (3:1-3). They could not see their arrogant freedom for what it really was, a thin cloak to cover idolatry. And their mistake was voiding what Paul had labored to instill in them. They were voiding the cross of Christ (1:17) by their worldly wisdom and knowledge.

Notice the significant factors Paul singled out. The repeated word "all" showed the direction of his argument. All experienced the great blessing of redemption from Egypt. A closer look at those blessings shows a clear comparison with the

Corinthians' blessing in Christ. The cloud and the sea equaled baptism "into Moses" (10:2).[9]

All the Israelites shared the same spiritual food and drink (10:3-4). The source of the sustenance was the "spiritual rock," Christ, the same source of spiritual food and drink for the Corinthians. Therefore, Paul's points of emphasis regarding Israel's blessing centered on their baptism and sustenance. The particular development of the food and drink aspects will come in chapter 11 concerning the Lord's table.

The concept of the "rock which followed them" (10:4) has much reference in Jewish tradition.[10] But Paul did not refer to the physical rock mentioned in the Jewish traditions. Paul's rock was "spiritual" and was the Messiah alone.[11]

Therefore, Paul did not present a typological relationship. For the apostle, the Messiah was actually present in the Old Testament event. Neither did Paul endorse the fanciful Jewish myth of an actual beehive-shaped rock that followed the Israelites over hill and dale.[12] Instead, Paul identified the preincarnate Christ with the angel of the Lord who went with Israel.[13] Thus, his thoughts were based on the historical provision that Christ made for the Israelites in the wilderness.

Paul's triple use of "spiritual" (10:3-4) referred to the supernatural origin of the nourishment to which the manna and water pointed. What was emphasized was the presence of the Messiah even with ancient Israel and the ensuing spiritual bless-

---

9. J. K. Howard, "Christ Our Passover: A Study of the Passover-Exodus Theme in I Corinthians," *Evangelical Quarterly* 41 (1969), p. 104. Howard notes the parallel between Jewish proselyte baptism and the passing through the Red Sea. The proselyte would pass from heathenism through baptism to the "promised land" of Judaism.

10. E. E. Ellis, *Paul's Use of the Old Testament* (Grand Rapids: Baker, 1957), pp. 66-70.

11. See R. G. Hammerton-Kelly, *Pre-Existence, Wisdom, and the Son of Man. A Study of the Idea of Pre-Existence in the New Testament* (Cambridge: University Press, 1973), p. 132.

12. E. E. Ellis, "A Note on First Corinthians 10:4," *Journal of Biblical Literature* 76 (1957), p. 56.

13. See Ex. 13:21; 14:19; 32:34; and Acts 7:30, 38; also Bruce, *1 and 2 Corinthians*, p. 91.

ings[14] and responsibility; a point much needed for the Corinthians. First Corinthians 10:1-4 was, therefore, designed to demonstrate the free participation of all Israel in the blessing of God. The purpose was to show that such participation still required consistent personal morality. That pattern of divine sovereignty and human responsibility was a part of the early Christian understanding. Whether in the Old or New Testaments, moral behavior was a requirement of the redeemed. That pattern of the messianic community in the Old Testament provided a rich source for those who saw the Person and plan of God to continue from the Old into the New Testament era. The pivotal and underlying concept is seen in 1 Corinthians 10:6, 11.

THE JUDGMENT ON THE FATHERS (10:5-11)

Even with all their spiritual and physical blessings, the Israelites were not pleasing to the Lord. How was His displeasure shown? By the fact that they "were laid low in the wilderness" (10:5).

Note the use of the Old Testament in 10:5. The words "laid low" are only here in the New Testament and in Numbers 14 in the Pentateuch of the Greek Old Testament. The passage Paul quoted (Num. 14:16) was a conjecture by Moses regarding what the Egyptians *might* say, were God to follow His plans to destroy Israel in the wilderness.

In the context of Numbers 14, the nation of Israel had just received the message of the twelve spies and was viewing with horror the impossible task of entering Canaan (Num. 14:1-4). Only the sudden appearance of the glory of God saved Joshua and Caleb from being stoned by the people (Num. 14:10). God then gave the verdict that He would destroy His nation and begin again with Moses (Num. 14:11-12).

At that point Moses interceded for Israel, pleading the

---

14. Bruce, *1 and 2 Corinthians*, p. 91; F. W. Grosheide, *Commentary on the First Epistle to the Corinthians* (Grand Rapids: Eerdmans, 1953), p. 221.

slander that would come upon the character of God if He were to carry out His plan of destruction. Numbers 14:16 was a theoretical slanderous remark that the Egyptians would make: God was not able to lead His people into the land, and consequently He had to destroy them in the desert. This quotation, then, was actually a sentence that Moses imaginatively put into the mouths of the scoffing Egyptians if they should hear that God had destroyed Israel.

Though all Israel had a common share in the blessing of God (1 Cor. 10:1-5), they were not all pleasing to God. The quotation from Numbers functioned as one of several historical examples (10:6) from which the Corinthians could benefit and learn.[15]

EXAMPLES OF ISRAEL TO AVOID (10:6-11)

The examples of the children of Israel were given for the church (10:6-11). The Old Testament context of those examples was Israel's idolatry that occurred during Moses' delay on Mount Sinai. The golden calf had been constructed, and Exodus 32:6 described the activities of Israel in her worship of it. Out of all the examples listed ("crave evil things" [10:6]; "idolators" [10:7]; immorality [10:8]; "try the Lord" [10:9]; and "grumble" [10:10]), why did idolatry get an Old Testament support from Exodus 32:6? Because it related directly to the Corinthian problem. They were prone to share ignorantly with the demons behind idols (10:20) and then bring their sinful state to the Lord's Supper in an "unworthy manner" (11:27).

The quotation illustrated the actions of a certain group within the nation ("some of them" [10:7]) in order to show the pleasures of Israel in their sin as well as the format of their sin: eating and immoral sport. The quotation was, therefore, an easily remembered and concise description of idolatrous acts

---

15. For example, Num. 14:20-23, 28-35 and Deut. 1:34-40. Though the phrase did not narrate the actual event, it was used as a convenient historical summary and, in fact, was true to the later facts of Israel's history.

and was included as a description of the idol feasts in Corinth.[16]

Paul viewed the events of Israel as historical realities that then became examples for his readers. The use of "happened" (10:6) needs to be compared with "happened to them as an example" (10:11). In the first instance, Paul was saying that the events of the Exodus became examples. That view was evidently a result of Paul's interpretive process, which saw the Old Testament as having direct implications for the present.

In the second instance, from Paul's perspective, those Old Testament events happened as examples; when they occurred, they were full of meaning that would transcend the following centuries. They were infused with a meaning for Paul's present. That was one reason "they were written" (10:11).

The link with Paul's present and the situation in Corinth was not so much the events of Exodus 32 as the attitude of God toward those events ("not well-pleased," 10:5). Therefore, the translations for the Greek words in 10:6 and 10:11 should be "examples" and "as examples," as in the NASB, rather than "types" and "typologically." Paul did not point to a prophetic type, somehow fulfilled in Corinth, but rather used the Old Testament events as warning ("instruction" [10:11]) based on the continuing and consistent attitude of God toward idolatry. God's principles of conduct as implied in the use of the five examples then became applicable to the Christians in Corinth. But with those examples a question might arise in the minds of the readers. What had Israel's past failure to do with Corinth?

Paul was presenting a finely tuned ethical demand leading up to the conclusion of 10:14. The quotation of 10:7 had proved only that some of the Israelites were idolaters, not that they were punished for it. The next verse (10:8) spoke of punishment. The quotation was designed to place idolatry in the context of judgment *within* the community of the redeemed. Paul used the vivid historical example of the events at Sinai to parallel the events in Corinth.

---

16. Bruce, *1 and 2 Corinthians*, p. 92. William F. Orr and James Arthur Walther, *I Corinthians* (New York: Doubleday, 1976), p. 246.

The cry of "all things are lawful" (10:23) for the redeemed had prompted Paul to counter with distinctions inherent within ancient, redeemed Israel. All things were not lawful. Some things, like idolatry, led to judgment. That was a direct, historical application of an Old Testament event to a New Testament ethical problem.

THINK YOU STAND? BEWARE! (10:12-13)

Before Paul made his final conclusion regarding the Corinthian problem with idol meats, he issued a warning to the "stronger"—the one "who thinks he stands" (10:12; see the pride problem already mentioned in 8:1, 9, 11-12). Paul next told his readers how to escape from failure (10:11-13). Because Israel's history was related to the end-time in Christ, Israel's salvation in the wilderness was closely linked to salvation in Christ.[17] That deeper significance of the history of Israel came as Paul reflected upon the teaching of the risen Christ.

In 10:13, Paul gave the key to avoiding the disqualification that Israel experienced—endure. The thought was this: (1) if you think nothing can trip you up, watch out (10:12); (2) since you have to watch out for stumbling, you are just like anyone else—subject to temptation; (3) therefore, admit your temptations, because God will provide a way of escape. The way of escape was not the way out of temptation, but was the way to "endure it" (10:13) without succumbing to sin. The particular way of escape in this context was the way of love over knowledge. The prematurely reigning (4:8) Corinthians needed to come down off their thrones and enter the real world, a world of temptations and deliverance.

WHEREFORE, FLEE IDOLATRY: OR SHARE IN DEMONS (10:14-22)

This section makes several links both forward and backward. The basic concepts are sharing, eating, and drinking. The eating and drinking relate to 10:7 and the problem of

---

17. Leonhard Goppelt, "Paul and Heilsgeschichte," ed. Mathias Rissi, *Interpretation* 21 (1967), p. 317.

idolatry, and they also look ahead to the problems with the Lord's Supper in chapter 11. The sharing idea looks back to 9:23 and Paul's great desire to share in the gospel, and it looks ahead to sharing in the Lord's Supper. Paul gave a strong command (10:14); his particular word for "therefore" was used only one other time in the letter (8:13). Paul had just said that God was faithful to make a way of escape from temptation (10:13). Now we see specifically what he had in mind: Corinthian idolatry. And the way of escape was to flee (a remedy also commanded by Paul in regard to immorality [6:18]).

Verses 15-22 are an exposition of Israel's wilderness failures (10:1-10) as applied to the Corinthians. Paul first proved that eating and drinking brought the participant into a close bond with Christ, the spiritual rock with whom Israel of old shared and partook (10:3-4), thereby introducing the specific idea of the Lord's Supper to be developed in chapter 11. The truth of becoming a sharer in the very body and blood of Christ should have led one away from idolatry. That was similar to Paul's argument regarding immorality in 6:15-17 ("Do you not know that your bodies are members of Christ?" [6:15]).

Next Paul gave an example of Jewish fellowship (10:18). In Paul's mind, the Old Covenant parallel with the Lord's Supper was not only manna and water in the wilderness, but also the sacrifices at the Temple in Jerusalem. The priests became "sharers in the altar."

But 10:19 shows that the idea of idols and sacrifices in Corinth had never left Paul's mind. Having established that the Lord's Supper and priestly sacrifice in Jerusalem brought the participants into a close bond with God (10:16-18), Paul applied the same truth to idols. Though neither the sacrifice nor the idol was "anything" (see 8:4), there were real demonic beings behind the sacrifices and images (10:20). Verse 20 quoted Deuteronomy 32:17: "They sacrificed to demons who were not God."

Verse 21 was another ethical, not actual, impossibility like the one seen in 6:15 ("Shall I then take away the members of Christ and make them members of a harlot? May it never be!"). Verse 22 alluded to Deuteronomy 32:21 ("They have made Me jealous with what is not God; they have provoked Me to anger with their idols.'') as Paul continued to use Israel as an example for the Corinthians.

APPLICATION (10:23—11:1)

ALL IS LAWFUL; BUT SEEK THE GOOD OF OTHERS (10:23-24)

Here Paul returned to the Corinthian assertions of being free to do ''all things'' (10:23; see 6:12). The issue was freedom along with profit and edification. Paul carefully balanced freedom and profit. ''All things'' were lawful for the person in Christ. But freedom was not the issue; edification was. Paul would neither diminish personal freedom nor violate the command for edification. Both were held in a tension that only resolved itself when a person glorified God (10:31) by seeking ''the profit of the many, that they may be saved'' (10:33).

REGARDING WHAT WAS SOLD (10:25-26)

Paul placed the purchase of idol meats into relationship with conscience (10:25). The word *conscience* occurs five times in 10:25-29. The question of idolatry was primarily centered on a Christian's eating sacrificial meat in an idol's temple (8:10), but here the question of conscience broadened to the eating of such meats purchased from the store. Paul supported his directive about not asking questions with a quotation from Psalm 24:1. No questions should be asked about where the meat came from, because everything was the Lord's possession. Secondary purposes such as use in idolatry could not dispossess the primary value of the meat as of the Lord and blessed by His creative hand.

EATING WHAT WAS SERVED (10:27-28)

Two cases were examined. The first concerned an invitation to dinner from an unbeliever.[18] No questions should be asked

18. For an example of an invitation to such a dinner, see G. H. R. Horsley, *New Documents Illustrating Early Christianity* (North Ryde, Australia: The Ancient History Documentary Research Centre, Macquarie University, 1981), pp. 5-9.

about the source of the food. The second case concerned the presence of someone who could not eat idol meats and knew that they were being served. When that person mentioned the fact, then no food should be eaten. Both cases were with regard to conscience's sake.

CORRECTIVE QUESTIONS CONCERNING CONSCIENCE (10:29-30)

Paul made his point by a question. If he was talking about the other person's conscience, why was his own freedom to eat being judged? The answer was that personal freedom was *not* being judged. Paul had made that clear throughout. The issue was not personal freedom; rather, at issue was the other person's conscience. Therefore, not eating meats was not a judgment against personal freedom but a conscious decision by the free person to limit the exercise of his freedom for the sake of another's conscience—the very thing Paul had illustrated from his own life in chapter 9. There was no basis for the weaker brother to make the strong feel guilty or condemned. The reason for not eating had nothing to do with freedom but lay in a different direction: the glory of God.

CONCLUDING EXHORTATION TO IMITATION (10:31—11:1)

Paul's conclusion in 10:31 shows what had been in his mind all along, the glory of God. But that was not a generalization. It had all the specifics of the particular situation at hand. The glory of God was seen by giving "no offense either to Jews or to Greeks or to the church of God" (10:32). The "no offense" relates to the same discussion of it in 8:9 and 9:12. Chapters 8-10 were focused on avoiding offense for all people so that the gospel could be furthered. That was cemented in 10:33, where the themes from chapters 8-9 (please all men, profit, and saved [9:19-23]) are reintroduced.

In 11:1, Paul repeated the call to imitation seen earlier in 4:16. There the call was to imitation of Paul as the proper view of leadership. Here the call was to imitation of Paul's glorification of God and furtherance of the gospel by self-limitation of freedom in order to become a servant of all.

7

THE TRADITIONS: KEPT AND UNKEPT

(11:2-34)

This section is closely aligned with chapters 8 through 10. It speaks of a minor problem in the exercise of freedom (women with uncovered head [11:3-16]). Paul had just commanded that all should glorify God and avoid causing offense to the church (10:31-32). But the issue of coverings for women was an example of something that was causing a minor offense (11:16). Paul devoted so much space to the problem because a more important issue was being clouded, the glory of God. All was to be done to His glory (10:31), but the head covering problem obscured that glory. Therefore, Paul began his discussion of the problem by an extended outline of the glory of God as mediated through Christ to the man and the woman.

But the main thrust of chapter 11 concerned an abuse of the Lord's Supper (11:17-34) that brought God's judgment upon the Corinthians (11:29-31). The themes of stumbling (10:31-33) and eating and drinking unworthily (10:1-5) reoccur.

MEN AND WOMEN IN WORSHIP (11:2-16)

The problem.

> Every man who has something on his head while praying or prophesying, disgraces his head. But every woman who has her head uncovered while praying or prophesying, disgraces her head; for she is one and the same with her whose head is shaved. (11:4-5)

The solution.

> But I want you to understand that Christ is the head of every man, and the man is the head of a woman, and God is the head of Christ. (11:3)

> Therefore the woman ought to have a symbol of authority on her head, because of the angels. (11:10)

THE LORD'S TABLE (11:17-34)

The problem.

> Therefore when you meet together, it is not to eat the Lord's Supper, for in your eating each one takes his own supper first; and one is hungry and another is drunk. (11:20-21)

> Therefore whoever eats the bread or drinks the cup of the Lord in an unworthy manner, shall be guilty of the body and the blood of the Lord. (11:27)

The solution.

> But let a man examine himself, and so let him eat of the bread and drink of the cup. (11:28)

The purpose.

> But if we judged ourselves rightly, we should not be judged.

PRAISE FOR KEPT TRADITIONS (11:2-16)

PRAISE FOR KEEPING THE TRADITIONS (11:2)

Verse 2 shows more fully what Paul had in mind by telling them to imitate him (11:1). To imitate him was to remember him "in everything, and hold firmly to the traditions" (11:2).

THE ISSUE OF ORDER AND DISGRACE OF HEAD (11:3-15)

This section on women's head coverings must be seen as a minor problem, one that could be finally dismissed with an appeal to common sense (11:13), the natural order (11:14-15), and church tradition (11:16). It was within the context of praise (11:2) rather than no praise (11:17), but it still caused Paul to bring his best theology to bear.

Headship (11:3-6). Paul outlined three steps of order; from God to Christ, Christ to men, and men to women (11:3). Paul spoke of a functional relationship—of the role each member played in relation to each other. The use of "head" in 11:4-13 is best taken in a literal sense of the head on the body. Paul did not speak of the essential nature of each member. Headship did not imply a superior nature. Christ was still divine, even though He was under the headship of God. Though the woman was under the headship of the man, that was a subordination of role, not of nature.

Men were not to have their heads covered (11:4). But Jews and Romans sometimes covered their heads in prayer; the Greeks did not.[1] Therefore, Paul was discussing a local issue especially focused on Greek culture. A man praying without a covering in Rome or Jerusalem might be criticized. In Corinth, however, bare heads for men in worship were the norm. But women needed a veil, just as they needed hair (11:5-6). It is clear that in Corinth, it was generally unacceptable for women to pray with uncovered heads. Those whose heads were shaved may have been involved in unusual religious rites.

Glories, creation, and equality (11:7-12). Two uses of "ought" (11:7, 10) prepared the foundation for understanding the "authority" of 11:10. Paul's thesis was that an uncovered head of the male related to his glory as the source (11:8) of the woman. It also related to the woman's role "for the man's sake" (11:9), showing how Paul viewed the woman as "the glory of man" (11:7) and the man as "the image and glory of God" (11:7). He spoke of functional glory related to the particular roles of male and female, not as related to man and woman's nature as created in the image of God (Gen. 1:27).

1. Hans Conzelmann, *1 Corinthians*, ed. James W. Leitch (Philadelphia: Fortress, 1975), p. 185. and *Encyclopaedia Judaica* (Jerusalem: Keter, 1972), s.v. "Headcovering."

The mention of angels (11:10) spoke of their presence at the assembly and the consequent need for decorum before such beings.[2]

That is supported in 11:11-12, where Paul showed the interdependence and equality of man and woman "in the Lord." God was the source of all; this was a guarded corrective by Paul to ward off any extremism that could result from misunderstanding the difference between subordination of role (a truth even within the Trinity [11:3*b*]) and essential equality. All had equal personal worth, though their roles may have differed.

Judge for yourselves (11:13-15). Paul then asked the Corinthians to judge on the basis of "nature" (11:14). Nature is to be taken in the sense of what was commonly and intuitively accepted. He simply asked them to admit that the most commonly accepted hairstyle was short for men and long for women. That was not to say that there never could occur situations in which a woman could have shorter hair and a man longer hair.

No such practice: the church of God (11:16). Paul ended the discussion with an appeal to commonly accepted church tradition, returning to the thoughts of 11:2. "Practice" (11:16) was closely aligned with "traditions" (11:2).

No Praise for Unkept Traditions: The Lord's Table (11:17-34)

Statement of the Problem (11:17)

Paul then turned to an unpraiseworthy problem. When the Corinthians assembled, it was "not for the better but for the worse." The worse would be defined as coming "together for judgment" (11:34).

Schisms (11:18-22*a*)

The accusation of "divisions" in the assembly (11:17-19) reflected the pervasive schisms noted from chapter 1 on. But the schisms had a surprising purpose—they showed the tested

2. J. A. Fitzmyer, "A Feature of Qumran Angelology and the Angels of I Cor. XI.10," *New Testament Studies* 4 (1957-58), pp. 48-58.

and approved ones (11:19). That was actually a blessing; who would want secret failures around? Those divisions would show who was approved, a question addressed with regard to the wise (2-3) and the true leaders (4). The specific division here showed who was despising the church of God (11:22).

Verse 20 clarified how they came together for the worse. Whatever they were doing, it was not for the Lord's Supper. They came together for judgment (11:34). However, they actually thought that they honored the Lord by selfishly eating and getting drunk in front of the poor. The Lord's Supper was not supposed to be a prideful display of wealth with a resultant neglect of the poor (11:21-22), but they, being so arrogant, did not see that they were despising the church of God.

The end of 11:22 returns to the opening words of this section in 11:17, showing that all of 11:17-22 was a description of the unpraiseworthy situation. In 11:23-26, Paul went on to explain the true meaning of the Lord's Supper in order to highlight how far removed they were from its intent. Then in 11:27-34, Paul explained how the Corinthians had been and would be subject to God's judgment for violating the holiness of the Supper.

THE TRUE NATURE OF THE LORD'S SUPPER (11:23-26)

Paul recounted what had been delivered (see 11:2, where Paul delivered the traditions to the Corinthians) to him by the Lord (11:23). The structure of this section is as follows:

> Narrative: 11:23-24*a*
> Quotation: 11:24*b*
> Narrative: 11:25*a*
> Quotation: 11:25*b*
> Editorial comment in preparation for application: 11:26

Verses 23-26 are the explanation ("for" [11:23]) of why Paul could not praise them (11:22).

The emphasis of that explanation was twofold: (1) the bread and cup were metaphors for the body and blood of Christ, and

(2) the Supper was to be held in remembrance of the Lord. Remembrance was a key element of the Jewish Passover (Ex. 12:14). But what was the Christian in Corinth to remember? The question was not what, but who. The Corinthians were to remember the Lord (stressed by the repeated "in remembrance of me" [11:24-25]). In practice, they were forgetting Him in their rush to indulge their wealth and appetites.

Paul had already likened the Christian life to the Passover feast (5:7-8) and the Israelites' journey through the wilderness after the Exodus from Egypt (10). But the Corinthians had forgotten their own exodus into purity (chaps. 5-7), and they had also forgotten the object of their gathering at the Lord's table.

The focus on the body and blood was explained in 11:26. The Lord's Supper was a proclamation of the death of Christ—not the fact that it happened but the fact of its divine and atoning nature. Also, it was an anticipation of His return ("until He comes," 11:26; see "until that day when I drink it new in the kingdom of God" [Mark 14:25]).

JUDGING THE BODY CORRECTLY (11:27-32)

Paul drew out the implications of the nature of the Lord's Supper for the Christian (11:27). At stake was not the wealthy or the poor in Corinth but the offense against the "body and the blood of the Lord." To be guilty in that manner meant to be guilty of forgetting the significance of the death of Christ ("remembrance" [11:24-25]), misrepresenting the death of Christ ("proclaim the Lord's death" [11:26]), and despising the ones for whom He died ("shame those who have nothing" [11:22]).

Next came the exhortation to test one's attitudes (11:28), because if one failed to test himself, there was a great penalty (11:29-31). Although "body" (11:29) could be seen to refer to the body of Christ (11:27), the surrounding context supports more strongly that it refers to the human body ("examine himself" [11:28]; many people were sick or dead [11:30]; "if we judged ourselves" [11:31; "when we are judged" [11:32]).

What went down the throat during the Lord's Supper could be "judgment" (11:29) if the body was improperly judged. Specifically, the issue was whether one was remembering the Lord or one's own appetite.

Was God really that serious about the sanctity and significance of His Son's table? Paul needed no theorizing; he pointed to "many among" them who were living or dead examples of God's attitude toward corruption of the Lord's Supper (11:30). The way out of such judgment was proper self-judgment (11:31). That sounds like a problem they also had regarding judging immorality in sexual (chap. 5), civil (chap. 6), marital (chap. 7), and religious (chaps. 8-10) contexts. They had trouble seeing sin for what it was, and they carried their lack of discernment right over into the Lord's table.

SUMMARY (11:33-34)

The Lord was potently present to judge the snobbish and hasty eaters of the Lord's table. The Supper was not for filling the belly, but for proclaiming the atoning death of Christ and sharing in His resurrected life until He returned. Though Paul had other items to address, he would wait to handle them in person (11:34; he had mentioned his return in 4:18-22). But the next item could not wait; it was doing too much damage to the church and its witness to unbelievers.

8

THE SOURCE AND WORTH
OF SPIRITUAL GIFTS

(12:1-31)

The following verses cover the material in 1 Corinthians 12-14 (chaps. 8 and 9 of this commentary).

The problem.

All are not apostles, are they? All are not prophets, are they? All are not teachers, are they? All are not workers of miracles, are they? All do not have gifts of healings, do they? All do not speak with tongues, do they? All do not interpret, do they? (12:29-30)

The solution.

For even as the body is one and yet has many members, and all the members of the body, though they are many, are one body, so also is Christ. (12:12)

On the contrary, it is much truer that the members of the body which seem to be weaker are necessary . . . that there should be no division in the body, but that the members should have the same care for one another. (12:22, 25)

But now abide faith, hope, love, these three; but the greatest of these is love. (13:13)

So also you, since you are zealous of spiritual gifts, seek to abound for the edification of the church. (14:12)

So then tongues are for a sign, not to those who believe, but to unbelievers; but prophecy is for a sign, not to unbelievers, but to those who believe. (14:22).

The purpose.

> Therefore, my brethren, desire earnestly to prophesy, and do not
> forbid to speak in tongues. But let all things be done properly and
> in an orderly manner. (14:39-40)

The force of chapter 12 was to help the Corinthians realize
that different gifts did not mean a different spiritual source or
a lesser worth (see 12:14, 19-20, 29-31). Functional diversity
did not annul spiritual unity.

INTRODUCTION: WHEN YOU WERE PAGANS (12:1-3)

Paul had left several unnamed items until his arrival (11:34),
but there was one item that could not wait. He did not want
them to be "unaware" (12:1) of "spiritual" (the word "gifts"
does not appear in the original Greek). The opening paragraph
(12:1-3) set up the significant role of the Spirit behind any
claim to the lordship of Christ, a seemingly obvious thought,
but one crucial to the development of Paul's argument
throughout chapters 12-14.

Usually throughout this letter, the "Now concerning"
phrases introduced a question that had come to Paul from Corinth. The same is probably true here, although the precise question is hard to pinpoint. At base it concerned the controlling
standards for knowing if someone was speaking by the Spirit
(12:3).

Paul used the Greek word for "spiritual" (12:1) in three different contexts in this letter. One way referred to spiritual
people. In 2:13, 15 it referred to spiritual people (see also Gal.
6:1). Chapter 3, verse 1 continued the 2:15 sense. In 14:37, the
"spiritual" one was closely aligned with the office of prophet.

A second use of spiritual is found in 9:11, where the word
signified the sowing of spiritual things (the same Greek words
refer to the spiritual forces of evil in Eph. 6:12). The neuter was
used once again in 15:46, "the spiritual."

The third usage referred to spiritual gifts (see Rom. 1:11). In
14:1, the word is clearly in the neuter gender and refers to

spiritual things, undoubtedly the gifts that had been at the forefront of the discussion throughout those chapters. That usage is clear enough to tip the scale in favor of seeing the 12:1 use to mean spiritual gifts rather than spiritual people. But the link was clearly close between the gifted and their gifts.

The issue was people proclaiming the lordship of Christ (12:3). But they did that according to various and differing gifts. Were they all of the Spirit? How could one really tell if a gift came from God? But most destructively, some implied that only a select number of gifts were of the Spirit, leaving the rest of the gifted people feeling left out of the Body ministry of Christ (12:15-16).

The first point Paul wanted to make concerned the religious past of his readers. He threw up before them their pagan past (12:2) and how they were "led astray to the dumb idols." The words indicate a diverse ("however you were led") involvement with idols—something they had not entirely shaken, as chapters 8-10 have shown. The main point was that they had been ignorantly drawn up into the worship of various idols and had given themselves over to proclaiming the lordship of many false gods. Paul discussed people first, before their gifts, in order to show the cause of their behavior. Various causes led them to follow idols. Paul would then make a conclusion about the singular and controlling cause and effect of Christian experience.

The criterion for spiritual gifts (in this specific context, the speaking gifts) was the proclamation of the lordship of Christ (12:3). General religious fervor and ecstasy alone were not proof of the presence of God's Spirit. Content ("Jesus is Lord"), not manner, was the key to discerning the truly spiritual.[1] "Jesus is Lord" was a general confession; chapters 12-14 will show the details of expressing the lordship of Christ. Did the Corinthians wonder how they could tell if something

---

1. C. K. Barrett. *The First Epistle to the Corinthians* (New York: Harper & Row, 1968), p. 281; and Birger Albert Pearson, *The Pneumatikos-Psychikos Terminology in 1 Corinthians* (Missoula, Mont.: Society for Biblical Literature, 1973), pp. 44-50.

was of the Spirit? Paul said that anything exalting the lordship of Christ was of the Spirit. Anything that did not do so was suspect.

The phrase "Jesus is accursed" (12:3) summed up all that the Spirit would not do or say. It is doubtful that Christians in Corinth actually said Jesus was accursed and thought they were worshiping God. The problem clearly centered on what some-one said when they were "speaking by the Spirit of God" (12:3). Was an ecstatic spiritual experience proof that the Spirit of God was speaking? Paul had answered no; content was the proof. The rest of chapters 12-14 unpacked the significance of that for their problem. Chapter 12 reinforced the essential, Spirit-sourced unity of all His diversely distributed gifts. Chapter 13 introduced the bond that kept all gifts operating in their proper direction. Chapter 14 applied those truths of unity, diversity, and love to the particular Corinthian problem with speaking in tongues.

DIFFERENCE IN GIFT DOES NOT MEAN A NON-SPIRIT SOURCE (12:4-11)

This section established the singular source of the Spirit behind each gift, addressing the Corinthian claim that certain gifts should be viewed with less honor than others. Paul's point in 12:1-3 was that the Spirit only exalted the lordship of Christ. In that light, 12:4-6 shows that the entire Trinity was involved in the ministry of spiritual gifts. "Varieties," the emphasis of 12:4-6, was balanced by three assertions of what was the "same" behind the "gifts," "ministries," and "effects": the Spirit, Lord, and God who "works all things in all persons" (12:6). Therefore, every Christian's gift manifested the Trinity at work. No one particular gift could be seen as a special or privileged class.

The Trinity was at work in all gifts (12:4-6). But toward what end? The Corinthians used some of their gifts without love and toward selfish ends. Therefore, Paul, in 12:7-10, expanded the Spirit's role in gifting to include its end—"for the common good" (12:7). The Greek word for "common good" was also used in 6:12; 7:35; and 10:23, 33. Verse 7 provides an excellent definition of the character ("manifestation of the Spirit") as well as the purpose of a spiritual gift.

Verse 8 begins a list of gifts (12:8-10) that defines *the common good.* All the way from knowledge to healing to tongues, only one purpose and end prevailed—benefiting others. That was the lesson many of the Corinthians needed to learn.

The repetition of "one Spirit" and "same Spirit" in 12:8-11 continues to support the basic problem concerning how to identify the Spirit in a gift. The Corinthians limited the Spirit's presence to a few more-flashy gifts, but Paul broadened that presence to include all the gifts. The Spirit not only effected the gifts, but He also distributed them (12:11). Therefore, one's gift was bestowed by the will of the Spirit and was not of human achievement. Paul's words in 4:7 apply here.

UNITY AND WORTH (12:12-31)

ONE BODY, MANY MEMBERS (12:12-14)

Verse 12 is the thesis statement of this section. The Body of Christ had many members, but all were unified by their being part of the Body. That raised the issue of how one entered into membership in the Body of Christ. Entrance came the same way for all: by baptism in the Spirit and by drinking of one Spirit (12:13). Diversity, such as ethnic (Jew or Greeks, see 7:18-19) or social (slaves or free, see 7:21-22) lines, had no bearing on entrance. Verse 14 re-emphasized verse 12. Therefore, the force of this section was to cause an acceptance of diversity, a realization of the source of such diversity (the Spirit), and, therefore, a realization of the resultant worth of each gift. Source, not function, determined membership and worth.

MANY MEMBERS: BUT ONE BODY (12:15-26)

The Corinthians had problems living with diversity, and as a result they had begun to seek a false unity under the guise of uniformity. In response, Paul stressed the many in a unified relationship within the Body of Christ (12:14). The illustrations Paul used in 12:15-26 exposed another problem in Corinth regarding spiritual gifts—discrimination. But that is what we would expect so far in light of the Corinthians' problems with wisdom, arrogance, and judgmentalism. Paul taught that the Spirit was to be seen as the criterion for identifying God's gifted people, not for evaluating the *worth* of their gifts. Worth was found in source, not function.

Function did not determine membership in the Body (12:15-17). Because the Spirit worked in many different ways, all those claiming the lordship of Christ were to be treated as equally gifted people (12:15-17). The figures in 12:15-16 presented the inferior member's seeking to be greater ("because I am not a hand" [12:15]; "because I am not an eye" [12:16]), a situation similar to that of chapter 7, where religious (7:18-19) and social (7:21) status was a cause of worry. Paul noted the necessity of diversity for a healthy body (12:17). Without diversity, vital functions would be lacking.

Diversity was God's idea (12:18). Verse 18 presented the most important reason for accepting diversity of functions within the Body of Christ. God had made the decisions "just as He desired." Who would dare to quibble with or try to alter that? There was a message for those who thought themselves either superior (eyes) or inferior (ears). Unfortunately, many Corinthians were unaware that their dissatisfactions with their gifts were a direct criticism of God.

The equality of all members (12:19-26). This section continued the figure of the necessity of having various different functions for a healthy body. But the focus now emphasized the specific practical problem; the superior assumed that they had no need for the other members. The stress was on "need" (12:21, 24) and "necessary" (12:22). Some in Corinth thought they had no need for "hands" or "feet," with the result that they denied *honor* where it was due (12:23-24).

Two points of view, both in error, had arisen. Some had the "foot and ear" complex and said they were not needed or important. Some had developed an "eye and hand' complex, saying they needed no one. But God had sovereignly incorporated diversity into the body so "there should be no division" and all "should have the same care for one another" (12:25). The presence of divisions has been seen before (1:10-11 and 11:18-19). Indeed, there were "weaker" (12:22) and more "seemly" (12:24) members in the body. Paul would even exalt some people's functions in the church in 12:28. But that relative importance of function had nothing to do with being more or less of a part of Christ's Body or with being worthy of honor. That was summed up in verse 26. Suffering and honor were the whole body's concern (note the repetition of "all the members").

SUMMARY (12:27-31)

This section returned to the question, begun in 12:12, of all being equal members of the Body of Christ. Verse 27 is the summary; all the Corinthians were collectively Christ's Body, and each individual was a member of it. The parts were determined by the whole. Paul already noted that individual function was a result of God's placement (12:18). He returned to that concept of placement in 12:28 ("appointed" is the same Greek word as "placed" in 12:18).

Paul next presented a partially numbered ("first," "second," "third") list of God's appointments in the church (12:28). Did the list reflect Paul's estimation of the importance of the appointments? In the immediate context, there is little support for that. However, the mere fact of the list shows Paul's emphasis on the priority of apostles, prophets, and teachers (each of which is numbered) over the other ministries that are not numbered.

Paul's point, however, was not to show particular importance of one ministry over another, but to show the bald fact of diversity (12:29-30). Seven times Paul said "all" in 12:29-30. Some in Corinth wanted everyone to have the same gifts. In 12:30, Paul left out "helps" and "administrations" from his list of 12:28, allowing swift movement of thought to the specific gift with which the Corinthians had problems. "All do not speak with tongues, do they? All do not interpret, do they?" The answer to those questions was expected to be no. All did not have the same gifts. Why? Paul had given several reasons earlier; health (12:17), sovereignty (12:18), mutual care and unity (12:25).

What Paul then had to do was fraught with potential contradictions. He had to encourage his readers to seek the "greater" (13:31) gifts, and then he had to explain what made some gifts greater. That would lead him first to discuss something even greater than gifts (chap. 13, especially v. 13). Then, with that foundation, he would discuss levels of greatness as applied to spiritual gifts (chap. 14, especially v. 5). But before that, Paul wanted to show them a way that was open to all, regardless of what gifts they had (12:31b).

9

THE PRACTICE OF SPIRITUAL GIFTS

(13:1—14:40)

THE BETTER WAY: LOVE (13:1-13)

EXTERNALS VERSUS LOVE (13:1-3)

Several dualisms are seen throughout this letter: (1) between the wisdom of man and that of God (1-4); (2) between knowledge and love (8-10); and, in 13:1, (3) between tongues and love. In chapter 13, Paul collected the majority of the Corinthians' problems under the solution of love.

Paul listed the noblest Christian virtues in 13:1-3 (tongues, prophecy, mysteries, knowledge, faith, alms, martyrdom). Surely the possession of any one of those attributes would be guarantee enough of a rich and profitable ministry. At least the Corinthians thought so. But Paul saw it another way and presented his initial case by three sets of if-then conditions. Each set was broken in the middle with a contrast ("but"). The first set (13:1) related to the ability to speak in a foreign (earthly or heavenly) language. The second set (13:2) related to the ability to speak from a wealth of heavenly ("mysteries") and earthly ("knowledge") teachings, and to the ability to believe ("faith") to the proverbial extent of moving mountains. The third set (13:3) related to the ability to give one's earthly possessions away to the poor and to give away one's own body to martyrdom.

Those were great acts of Christian faith—on the surface. Paul added a crucial contrast to each of those three conditions: "but do not have love." Immediately all the great abilities and deeds had to be seen in a new light. They could exist in two modes, with and without love. No longer could one marvel at his or another's gift or act. An accompanying question would have to be asked: Did it come with love? What if it did not? Paul's last part of each set answered that question.

Without love the great speaking gifts were noise (13:1), and the speakers were nothing (13:2). Without love the great acts of charity and witness brought the giver and witness no profit. Note that Paul did not say that the gifts or deeds did not profit others; that was left unaddressed. Paul's focus was on what accrued to the one speaking or acting. That one received nothing because he was nothing. This focus shows that the Corinthians were interested in having certain gifts for their own benefit and profit. Paul tried to correct that self-centered approach more fully in chapter 14. Actually, the entire letter seems to have been one grand attempt by Paul to correct Corinthian selfishness by explaining the power and implications of the wisdom, purity, power, and love that was founded in the cross of Christ.

The selection of subjects in this chapter is very closely aligned with the particular problems dealt with in this letter.[1] Speaking with tongues was the particular spiritual gift being misused in Corinth (14), and it headed Paul's list in 13:1. To have "the gift of prophecy" and to "know all mysteries and all knowledge" (13:2) was the central topic of the Corinthians' problems (with knowledge and leadership factions) in the first four chapters. Properly understood, prophecy would become the loving alternative to correcting the problem with tongues (14:5). Chapter 12 clustered those gifts as "knowledge, faith, healing, miracles, and prophecy." The order in chapter 14 is revelation, knowledge, prophecy, teaching. In 13:3, Paul mentioned the good deed of giving away goods for the poor, the very subject with which he will close this letter (16:1-4). Therefore, many of the items in the list of 13:1-3 seem tailor-

---

1. William F. Orr and James Arthur Walther, *1 Corinthians* (New York: Doubleday, 1976), p. 290; C. K. Barrett, *A Commentary on the First Epistle to the Corinthians* (New York: Harper & Row, 1968), p. 297.

made for the Corinthian situation. The next section (13:4-7) continued with that same pertinence for Corinth.

LOVE'S BEHAVIOR (13:4-7)

This section introduced a change of style from 13:1-3. Here we find, not a definition of love, but how love operated in the everyday aspects of life. Paul portrayed love as a person, one who was kind and patient. Love was at the heart of all the good qualities listed. If someone was patient, love was behind it. If someone was kind, love was there. Love, then, was the heart of the wise way of life.

In this section, several of the qualities of love were especially relevant to the Corinthian situation. Patience (13:4) certainly was not being given to the weaker brother of chapter 8 or issuing from the gluttons of chapter 11. "Jealous" (13:4) related to the "jealousy and strife" of 3:3. "Brag" (13:4) was a Corinthian pastime (4:7; 5:6). "Arrogant" (13:4) was almost the key word for the Corinthian problem (4:6, 18; 5:2; 8:1). "Seek its own" (13:5) mirrored "seek his own" (10:24). "Take into account a wrong" (13:5) referred back to the whole problem of lawsuits in chapter 6 (see 6:7-8 especially). "Rejoice in unrighteousness" (13:6) raised the specter of the Corinthians' boasting in the great immorality of chapter 5.

But the items in 13:4-7 also transcended the particular Corinthian problems. Verse 7, in particular, widely expanded the limits of love in life. That fourfold statement summed up all the qualities in 13:4-6. Two words with much overlapping sense ("bears, endures") framed the inner two words ("believes, hopes"). Four times the words "all things" punctuate the sense. The four phrases relate but two singular points. First, love would not collapse into hatred in the face of, for example, impatience, jealousy, boasting, arrogance, or insult. Second, love covered all things with faith and hope. It saw life, the good and the bad, from the perspective of faith and hope.

EXTERNALITY AND PRESENT PARTIALITY OF LOVE (13:8-13)

This section ushers in another change of tone. Verses 1-7

showed love from the perspective of wisdom in daily life. In 13:8-13, daily life was replaced with the radical change brought by eternity. Paul set love and gifts in relation to one aspect: permanence. Gifts were not eternal. They were provisional manifestations of the Spirit and would pass away. "Love never fails" (13:8) was Paul's thesis. The following context shows that "fails" meant eternally (the "abide" of v. 13). In contrast with love's permanence, prophecy, tongues, and knowledge would end. The change from "done away" to "cease" and back again is difficult to explain. It may simply be stylistic and carry no special interpretive weight. The time of the end of those gifts, however, was clearly delineated in 13:9-12.

Verse 9 explains ("for") when all the gifts will be done away with and why. They will pass away because they are not "the perfect" (13:10); they are "in part" (13:9) and "partial" (13:10) ministries. That was a perspective the already full and reigning (4:8) Corinthians were overlooking. They were not in the kingdom yet, and their gifts, while wonderful, were not perfect. Verse 10 introduces the time when gifts will pass away. It will be "when the perfect comes." The tenses of 13:9-10 show that Paul was still in the "in part" time. In verse 12, he said "now we see in a mirror dimly." Paul did not immediately explain what he had in mind for the perfect. His interest was to illustrate *how* its coming affected the Corinthians' view of their gifts. His illustration was of a child and a man.

The straightforward point of 13:11 was that maturity has a radical effect on immaturity. In this case it resulted in doing "away with childish things." "Did away" is from the same Greek word as "done away" (13:8). Clearly the doing away with childish things was to be equated with the time of the doing away of the gifts. That was illustrated by Paul as the time of maturity brought on by the coming of the perfect. Thus, Paul placed the exercise of all the gifts in the time of the imperfect and for the immature children, in which he included himself, as the next verses show.

Again Paul resorted to a figure of speech to convey his point (13:12). The mirror gazing was for "now"; the "face to face" was for "then." Paul used seeing and knowing to sum up Christian ("we") religious experience both now and then. The now and then times must match up with the child and man states of 13:11. Paul placed himself and all Christians in the partial, child, and dim mirror period. That was the period of the gifts. Another period awaited. That was the period of the perfect, of becoming a man, of face-to-face sight and knowledge. That would spell the end of the gifts.

When is that period of the perfect? Paul was not in it and was quite content to exercise his "in part" gifts and knowledge (see, e.g., 14:18). I believe that absence of gifts coupled with full knowledge (13:12) could only describe the church's face-to-face experience with her Lord at His coming.

To conclude his argument, Paul returned to the present ("but now" [13:13]) to note that faith, hope, and love were abiding. Love was the greatest, however. Paul had already shown the relationship of faith and hope to love in 13:7. Love believed (faith) and hoped (hope) the best from God's perspective. The triad of faith, hope, and love is seen in Romans 5:3-5 and 1 Thessalonians 1:3; 5:8. Love was "greatest," referring back to 12:31, where Paul encouraged his readers to seek the "greater gifts." Chapter 14 will be a specific application of the greater quality of love to the seeking of the greater gifts. But love alone was qualified to be a better way.

SUMMARY OF CHAPTERS 12—14

Chapter 12 taught that all spiritual gifts were worthy of equal honor. Therefore, the Corinthians should not exalt one gift over another. Chapter 13 showed the necessity of love's operating behind each gift. Therefore, the Corinthians were not to exercise their gifts without love. Chapter 14 taught that the application of love in the specific gift of tongues would always equal edification. Therefore, that gift should not be exercised without edification.

THE BETTER WAY APPLIED TO GIFTS (14:1-40)

THESIS: PURSUE LOVE AND SEEK PROPHECY (14:1)

In this chapter, Paul applied the truths of chapters 12-13 to the Corinthians' problem with speaking in tongues. Paul had mentioned the pursuit of spiritual gifts several times (12:31; 14:1, 12). Evidently one could pray for a gift (14:13). However, Paul's "desire earnestly spiritual gifts" spoke to the community's attitude toward gifts, not to the individual's own desires for possessing this or that gift.

In 14, we see what Paul meant by the greater gifts. A gift's greatness was judged by its ability to edify. That was why chapter 14 revolved around tongues and prophecy. *Prophecy* was one of the greater gifts, because it achieved greater edification.

THESIS APPLIED: SEEK EDIFICATION (14:2-19)

The essence of greatness (14:2-5). Verse 2 began an explanation of why they should give special time to seeking prophecy. Paul's first point was that of the inaccessibility of tongues; it was spoken "to God," "in his spirit" and was composed of "mysteries," with the result that "no one understands."

The contrast of prophesy (14:3) was that the whole process became accessible to human beings and resulted in "edification and exhortation and consolation." Verse 4 summed up the thought. The issue was self-edification versus church edification. That raised the key issue for the exercise of tongues: within the assembly (14:19, 23, 26).

As if to ward off an extreme reaction against tongues, Paul affirmed the worth of the gift of tongues (14:5). Chapter 12 had already established the equal worth of all the gifts, because their source was in God. It had also clearly affirmed the diversity of gifts as being of God's own design (12:28-30). Therefore, Paul's wish for all to speak in tongues and prophesy was a rhetorical device designed to support the high worth of tongues, but also to show the greater desirability of prophecy.

The criterion of edification, however, determined the use and priority of prophecy.[2] When tongues were interpreted,

---

2. Wayne A. Grudem, *The Gift of Prophecy in 1 Corinthians* (Washington, D. C.: Univ. Press of America, 1982). Grudem presents a most thorough examination of prophecy in Corinth regarding its form, content, and manner.

they, too, were of high worth (14:5), opening up the solution to the problem with tongues. The problem was not with the gift itself but with its place in the edification process. It was incomplete in itself and needed accompanying interpretation. The development of the need for interpreted tongues took Paul through the end of this chapter.

"But now"—the profit theme (14:6). Paul next introduced four aspects of profitable speaking. Tongues brought no "profit" in and of themselves. Profit was another way of speaking of edifying (14:4-5) and also referred to the same concept in 13:3. A Christian act or gift brought no profit apart from love's extension into the lives of others. The four categories ("revelation," "knowledge," "prophecy," and "teaching") were the building blocks of profit.

Even though it is of interest to the modern reader to have had Paul go into how those four categories actually operated, his purpose was not to discuss the gifts themselves (the specific operation and expressions of the gifts is not at all a subject of interest in 1 Corinthians). His purpose was to demonstrate the indispensability of understanding for profit and edification. That purpose led Paul into another illustration.

Musical instruments (14:7-9). Verses 7-9 and 10-12 form two units of illustrations, each ending with "so you also" and an application of the particular illustration. Verses 7-9 assume the thoughts of verse 6. "Distinction" of tone was vital if what was played was to be "known" (14:7). From the flute and harp, Paul moved to the bugle (14:8). With an "indistinct sound," the intended message would be obscured.

Verse 9 brought the application. "Clear" speech alone could bring knowledge. Clear speech related to the four gifts mentioned in 14:6 and was vital for profit in the church. That was very pertinent to the way Paul began the entire discussion of spiritual gifts in 12:1-3. Because the problem was knowing if someone was speaking by the Spirit of God, Paul immediately focused his readers on the standard of content (12:3)—that which could be known. The same idea is in 14:7-9. Tongues, without interpretation, could not give something to be known.

Knowledge was, therefore, the foundation of edification.

Zeal and edification (14:10-12). These verses continue Paul's illustrations of the need for a known sound by showing how languages are communicated in either meaningful or barbaric ways. Who would want to come across as a barbarian (14:11)? In that light, Paul encouraged the Corinthians to let their zeal for spiritual gifts direct them toward an equal zeal for edification (14:12); "edification of the church" (14:12) was the opposite of "speaking into the air" (14:9).

Interpret tongues: help the mind (14:13-19). Paul used the strongest Greek word for a conclusion in 14:13. Interpretation must follow tongues speaking. Verse 14 explained the personal loss of the one who spoke in tongues: the "mind is unfruitful." The mind needed to receive the profit of understanding. The benefit from tongues was not accessible to the mind. Therefore, the phrase "edifies himself" (14:4) should be taken to refer to edification of the nonrational part of the person—the realm of the spirit (14:14). That was an area of edification outside of Paul's interests at this point and was even a detriment to church edification (14:17).

The Spirit was recognized in Corinth, but the role of the mind was in need of emphasis (14:15, note the repeated "mind also"). Use of uninterpreted tongues left the "ungifted" person in the dark and unedified (14:16-17). Like the poor who were left at the Lord's Supper without any food (11:22), the ungifted were left without knowledge while the gifted enjoyed their spiritual feasting.

Paul returned to his praise of tongues on the one hand and his "in the church" desires on the other (14:18-19). Paul presented the godly balance between the gift of tongues in and of itself and its exercise in the church. Why did he want to speak words with his mind (14:19)? Because he wanted to instruct "others also." The foundation of Paul's argument was that tongues could not bring that kind of edifying profit and instruction. The following are some of the different ways Paul characterized the misuse of tongues: "no one understands" (14:2); "edifies himself" (14:4); no profit (14:6); "speaking into the air'' (14:9); "be a barbarian" (14:11); and "mind is unfruitful" (14:14).

BE MATURE: TONGUES ARE FOR JUDGMENT (14:20-25)

Call for mature thinking (14:20). These verses bring a change of tone introduced by the direct address ("brethren") concerning being mature. The clear implication was that the Corinthians' present way of thinking about tongues was considered childish by Paul, and that he was presenting the mature perspective.

The standard of mature thinking (14:21-25). Verse 21 presented the mature view of tongues by quoting from Isaiah 28:11-12.[3] In that passage, unintelligible tongues were a divine message of correction that was frustrated by a disobedient response.

The final phrase in Paul's text ("even so they will not listen to me") implied that the dullness of hearing was in the face of the foreign tongues. But the phrase in Isaiah was a retrospective look to the days when God had spoken through His prophets before He had to bring the judgment of Assyria. Thus, the quotation as used by Paul took up two strands of the Isaiah passage, foreign tongues and disobedience, but followed the Greek Old Testament version by directly linking hardness of hearing with the tongues.

In the Old Testament context, Isaiah 28:16 must not be overlooked. That was the cornerstone text so often used to refer to God's great act of salvation through Jesus. Tongues were, therefore, the sign of judgment that surrounded the cornerstone. In the Old Testament context, the prophet gave warning to the inhabitants of Jerusalem that, for all their efforts to save themselves, they would be broken for their offenses against God. The foreign tongue was the language of the Assyrians soon to be heard at the downfall of Jerusalem. Paul gave his explanation of the Old Testament passage in 14:22.

---

3. This quotation is one of several in the New Testament that incorporate the phrase *"says the Lord."* See E. E. Ellis, *Paul's Use of the Old Testament* (Grand Rapids: Baker, 1981), pp. 107-13.

Tongues were for a sign, a sign of God's delayed but righteous judgment. The people had been offered rest but did not listen. Therefore, the next message they would receive from God would be unavoidable judgment. Paul saw a correspondence between the speaking of God through the Assyrians and His speaking through the Corinthian Christians. That correspondence centered on the concept of sign for both Israel and the church. The Assyrian tongue was a sign of divine judgment and impending destruction for Jerusalem. As God had spoken a message to Israel through the sign of the Assyrian tongue, so also He was speaking a message to Israel through Christian glossolalia.[4]

Some say that Paul used a passage having nothing to do with the ecstatic utterances he was discussing.[5] But that assumes that the utterances were ecstatic rather than the foreign languages seen, for example, in the book of Acts. If the utterances were human languages, then Paul's use of Isaiah 28:11-12 would be within the bounds of the Old Testament context.[6] That, combined with Paul's shared sense of a divine, but rejected, message, serves to further his harmony with the Old Testament.

Tongues were for a sign to "unbelievers," and prophecy was for believers.[7] That latter point had already been stressed several times in this chapter. The tongues of the Isaiah quotation gained a bad response—the people would "not listen." Paul concluded that the tongues in Corinth would produce the

---

4. T. W. Manson, "St. Paul in Ephesus: The Corinthian Correspondence," *Bulletin of the John Rylands Library* 26 (1941), p. 115.
5. S. L. Edgar, "Respect for Context in Quotations from the Old Testament," *New Testament Studies* 9 (1962-63), p. 57; C. H. Dodd, *According to the Scriptures* (London: Nisbet, 1952), p. 83.
6. Willis W. Wantock, "Speaking in Tongues in First Corinthians." Th.M. thesis, Dallas Theological Seminary, 1970.
7. Wayne Grudem, "I Corinthians 14:20-25: Prophecy and Tongues as Signs of God's Attitude," *The Westminster Theological Journal* 41 (1979), pp. 381-96; B. C. Johanson, "Tongues, a Sign for Unbelievers?: A Structural and Exegetical Study of I Corinthians XIV.20-25," *New Testament Studies* 25 (1979), pp. 180-203.

same negative response; therefore, tongues had only a negative response of unbelief to offer.

In that sense, tongues were a sign for unbelievers; that is, for those who were so hardened in their unbelief that they would not respond to God. The sign for such a group was one of judgment. In Isaiah, the sign of tongues was certain Assyrian destruction of Jerusalem. In Corinth, tongues would bring unbelief; prophecy would bring belief. Who would want, then, to exercise a gift that was designed as a sign to those too hardhearted to repent?[8] Unbelief would only be aggravated by the phenomenon.

The quotation asserted that tongues were not a final effort to gain repentance before destruction, but rather a sign that talking was at an end and irrevocable judgment was at hand. Such was the bald intention of the phenomenon of tongues. The Corinthians lacked that mature perspective about their tongues speaking. Verses 23-25 developed the functions of tongues and prophecy from that perspective.

Paul linked the derisive response of the unbeliever, or unskilled, to the presence of uninterpreted tongues (14:23). The result, similar to the Isaiah context, was negative. And in contrast to the mocking response to tongues by the unbeliever is his response to prophecy (14:24-25). His opinion moved from madness to a conviction and sense that God was present. Paul embraced both the conviction unto salvation of an unbeliever and the conviction within salvation of an ungifted (in the gift of tongues) Christian. That described edification and evangelism, a burden of all Paul's actions (9:19-22). Now we see why Paul desired that all would prophesy (14:5), because all would then be involved in the wonderful ministry of conviction and worship described in 14:14-25. If all spoke in tongues (14:23), that great ministry would never be realized.

Paul would soon (14:26-27) modify that basic view of tongues by the addition of an interpreter. That addition moved

---

8. Hans Conzelmann, *1 Corinthians,* ed. James W. Leitch (Philadelphia: Fortress, 1975), p. 285.

the effect of tongues from unintelligibility to intelligibility, from judgment to prophecy and edification. Only that way could the gift of tongues gain acceptability for public use in the church.

The concept of tongues was approached in chapter 14 from one perspective only, its relation to edification. In showing the primary ideas surrounding the original use of tongues (irreversible judgment directed to Israel), Paul showed how incompatible that was with the work of the assembled church. The unbeliever, when given the sign, would be hardened in his unbelief: he would not listen.[9] Paul called that understanding of tongues "mature" (14:20).

WHEN YOU ASSEMBLE, EDIFY (14:26-33*a*)

All for edification (14:26). "When you assemble" refers back to the many mentions of the Corinthians' coming together in chapter 11:17-18, 20, and 33-34. Paul summed up ("what is the outcome then") the exercise of the various things done in the assembly in one phrase: "Let all things be done for edification." Earlier in the chapter, edification was defined by how clear the message was (14:9). Here edification was viewed from another but related aspect, assembly order.

Order for tongues (14:27-28). Paul advised a limit (three) and an order ("in turn") for tongues speaking. If no interpreter was present, the individual was asked to remain silent and do his speaking to himself and God. That most likely related to tongues speaking in private homes.

Order for prophets (14:29-33*a*). A limit was also placed on prophets (three [14:29]) and their order ("one by one" [14:31]). No interpreter was needed, but the others were to "pass judgment" (14:29) upon the content of the revelation. Just as with tongues, so with prophecy: content, not fervor, was the standard for the presence of the Lord. The spirits of the prophets were under their control (14:32); there was no ex-

9. J. P. M. Sweet, "A Sign for Unbelievers: Paul's Attitude to Glossolalia," *New Testament Studies* 13 (1967), p. 242.

cuse for uncontrolled prophetic outbursts. Verse 33 explained that further. Peace, not confusion (uncontrolled outbursts), was God's way. But there was also another problem with people speaking in inappropriate ways, as 14:34-36 explained.

THE ALL-CHURCHES POSITION ON SILENT WOMEN (14:33*b*-36)

Major English and Greek versions support taking 14:33*b* as the first part of the sentence that continues into 14:34 (NEB, RSV, NIV, Aland, United Bible Societies). That placed the discussion of women into a universal, all-church custom.

Women were not permitted to speak in the assembly (14:34). Whether such speaking referred to tongues, prophecy, or simple asking of questions (14:35), it was not allowed. In that light, the praying and prophesying mentioned in 11:5 is best seen as done outside the formal assembly. The question was not that women could not have those gifts, but simply that they were not to be exercised in the assembly, much as untranslated tongues were not to be exercised in the assembly.

The silence of women was simply an extension of the silence of males that Paul commanded earlier. Without a translator, a tongues speaker was to "keep silent" in the church (14:28). When a revelation was made to another prophet, the first prophet was to "keep silent" (14:30). The point was to give a chance for all to learn (14:31), the extension of which would have to proceed in the home for married women (14:35). The male prophets' spirits were subject to themselves (14:32). The women, following the Old Testament order of creation, were to be subject to their husbands (14:34). Therefore, Paul's discussion of silence, learning, and subjection of women followed very logically out of his discussion of the same subjects for men. To end that discussion, Paul laid claim once again to common church practice, much as he did with the question of women in 11:3-16. But that claim carried more than a little bit of sarcasm as Paul asked them if they considered themselves the sole source and recipients of God's Word (14:36).

THE LORD'S COMMAND AND A FINAL SUMMARY (14:37-40)

Lest any think that Paul was giving his personal opinion, he stated that he had delivered the "Lord's commandment" (14:37) and that a spiritual person would recognize it as such. Paul was not being sarcastic here, however. He was subjecting himself to the same rules he had laid down (by the Lord's commandment) in 14:29. Paul as prophet gave what he claimed to be a commandment of the Lord, spoken by revelation of the Spirit. He then asked for the other prophets and spiritually mature to pass judgment. So great was his confidence that he spoke for the Lord, however, that he dismissed any negative vote as not worthy of recognition (14:38).

His final words on the subject keep the balance that could so easily have been broken. The Corinthians were to "desire earnestly to prophesy" (14:39), thus achieving the edification of love. They were also, however, not to "forbid to speak in tongues," a potentially severe backlash in light of the problems created by the misuse of tongues apart from interpretation. Possibly, the forbidding of tongues was what initiated the question of 12:1 in the first place. Certainly what Corinth did not need was the development of "for-tongues" and "against-tongues" factions. They had enough schisms already. For the time being, Paul commanded that "all things be done properly" (the aspects of edification, 12:1—14:25) and "in an orderly manner" (the patterns of order, 14:26-36).

10

THE QUESTION OF THE RESURRECTION

(15:1-58)

INTRODUCTION

THE RESURRECTION

The problem.

> Now if Christ is preached, that He has been raised from the dead, how do some among you say that there is no resurrection of the dead? (15:12)

> But if there is no resurrection of the dead, not even Christ has been raised; and if Christ has not been raised, then our preaching is vain, your faith also is vain. (15:13-14)

The solution.

> But now Christ has been raised from the dead, the first fruits of those who are asleep. (15:20)

> Now I say this, brethren, that flesh and blood cannot inherit the kingdom of God; nor does the perishable inherit the imperishable. (15:50)

The purpose.

> Therefore, my beloved brethren, be steadfast, immovable, always abounding in the work of the Lord, knowing that your toil is not in vain in the Lord. (15:58)

The Corinthians had a problem with the resurrection of the believer. They bluntly said that there was "no resurrection of the dead" (15:12). But they had not seen the implications of that position for Christ's own resurrection. Therefore, in this chapter Paul labored to show how closely the resurrections of the believer and of Christ were tied together. Resurrection was a unity and an all-or-nothing package. Christ's resurrection could not be an exception.

The progression of thought throughout the chapter is as follows. The resurrection of Christ was integral to the gospel (15:1-11). Without the resurrection, salvation was not a reality (15:12-19). But if Christ was resurrected, then the believer would be also (15:20-28). Without the resurrection, motivation for godly living evaporated (15:29-34). Because the resurrection would bring its own special kind of glory (15:35-49), a changed body was a necessity for all who would enter the kingdom (15:50-58).

Two major points were established: (1) everyone needed to change into the "imperishable" in order to inherit the kingdom (15:50); and (2) the hope of resurrection should lead to being "steadfast" and to knowing that one's work was not "in vain in the Lord" (15:58). The first point addressed the Corinthian misconception that they were already reigning as kings in the kingdom, or at least ready to enter it as they were (4:8). The second point ministered to the discouragement that was creeping into the church in light of the mistaken notions about the resurrection.

I MAKE KNOWN: THE GOSPEL (15:1-2)

The section of 15:1-11 stressed the centrality of the resurrection for the gospel. It began and ended with references to the presentation and acceptance of the gospel in Corinth (15:1, 11). The outline of that gospel was twofold: (1) Christ died (15:3), and (2) Christ was raised (15:4). Although Paul gave proof for each of those two points, the second, concerning resurrection, received the most support.

In addition to the Scriptures (15:4), Paul marshalled the support of Cephas, the twelve, a crowd of over five hundred, James, the apostles, and Paul himself. Why all that proof? Because resurrection in general was doubted in Corinth (15:12), though it is not clear that the Corinthians actually doubted Christ's resurrection. Paul nowhere implied or specifically addressed that.

But whereas the Corinthians may not have seen the ramifications of their doubts for Christ's resurrection, Paul certainly had. Christ's resurrection was not an isolated event, but the opening of the door to the believer's resurrection. Any hope of the believer for resurrection was totally dependent upon the fact of Christ's own resurrection. That was why Paul began with the gospel and with the resurrection at its core. Hundreds had witnessed the resurrected Christ. Did that not have implications for the Corinthians' theories about the acceptability or nonacceptability of resurrection?

The gospel was defined by four aspects. It was preached to them, they received it, they stood by it, and they were saved by it (15:1-2). That gospel was the sum of their salvation. Paul added a startling condition ("if"); all could end up vain if they did not hold fast the entire message (15:2). Paul would use himself as an example of one who did not let his commitment become vain (15:10). He saw the whole Christian enterprise as vain without the resurrection (15:14). He would also end this chapter by saying that their labors were not in vain. That illuminates the problem at hand. It was not just speculative; it was eroding the will to persevere by teaching that Christian hope was only good for this life (15:19).

Clearly the doctrinal problem Paul was addressing had serious consequences. They had been committed to the gospel. Were they altering that original commitment?

FOUNDATIONS OF THE GOSPEL (15:3-11)

In light of the crucial nature of the originally delivered gospel (15:1-2), Paul outlined the foundations of the gospel, emphasizing the fact of Christ's resurrection.

In 15:3-11, Paul established the truth of the gospel (15:3-8) and his own worth as a reliable witness of the risen Lord (15:9-10). His reference to himself as "one untimely born" (15:8) is an ugly way to describe his conversion. The concept of an abortion or miscarriage is seen in the Old Testament (Num. 12:12, Eccles. 6:3, and Job 3:16). But Paul's meaning here must be discerned from his explanatory ("for") sentence in 15:9. He was, unlike the other apostles, born again directly out of his own intense persecution of the church of God. Paul had been attacking the Lord Himself (Acts 9:4-5). That was what made Paul, in his opinion, the last of all (15:8) and the "least of the apostles" (15:9).

In spite of his call in the midst of persecuting the church, Paul claimed the "grace of God" (15:10) in letting his life be what it was, both the bad and the good. His point was that, regardless of his past life, when he was born again he did not take lightly the grace of God offered to him. He "labored even more than all of them" in cooperation with the grace of God.

What might seem like a personal, and somewhat irrelevant, digression into his past life was really an important foundation for supporting Paul's claim to be a reliable witness of the risen Lord. Some even see a defense against slander from Paul's opponents.[1] But the end of the matter was that whether it was Paul or other apostles, they all preached the same gospel, and the Corinthians believed in it. Paul would then expand the implications of those foundational truths for the problem at hand.

IMPLICATIONS OF DENYING CHRIST'S RESURRECTION (15:12-19)

This section showed the bad things that would happen if the resurrection were false. The problem was revealed by a question (15:12). Paul did not argue that Christ's resurrection was indispensable for the believers—he assumed it. Resurrection was a seamless whole; do away with the believer's resurrection and you do away with Christ's.

1. C. K. Barrett, *The First Epistle to the Corinthians* (New York: Harper & Row, 1968), pp. 344-45.

What could those Corinthians who denied the resurrection have meant? They may have believed that after death there was only eternal spiritual existence, or that only the living would be glorified in eternal bodies when Christ came. At any rate, their specific ideas were not spelled out by Paul.

What he emphasized was "how" (15:12), in light of Christ's having been raised, anyone could say there was no resurrection. Only those who had not connected personal resurrection to Christ's resurrection could take that position. And that position was creating the attitudes noted in 15:19, 32, a pessimistic and "this is all there is" view of life. No wonder Paul ended this chapter with an exhortation that Christian labor was not in vain. The resurrection of Christ was then linked to the fiber of their faith (15:13-19). If there were no resurrection, several dimensions of faith would topple. Christ's resurrection would not exist (15:13), Paul's preaching would have been vain (15:14, the very thing he denied in 15:10), and the Corinthians' faith would have been vain. And worse, Paul's vain preaching would have been a false witness against God (15:15).

In 15:16-19, Paul referred back (15:16; see 15:13) to the absence of Christ's resurrection and drew another implication from it: worthless faith meant no forgiveness (15:17). It also meant that the unforgiven Christian dead had perished (15:18). Verse 19 drew the awful conclusion: hope was limited to "in this life" and was cut off from forgiveness and eternal reward. Paul had come full circle from 15:2. In no way could the gospel message have brought salvation if it had not brought resurrection. Christ's death for sins (one pillar of the gospel message, 15:3) was meaningless without His resurrection from the dead.

SOLIDARITY AND SUBORDINATION DESCRIBED (15:20-28)

In 15:1-11, Paul had demonstrated the centrality of the resurrection for the gospel message. In 15:12-19, he had shown the awful consequences for the Corinthians' salvation if the resurrection were denied. In 15:20-28, he began to explain how the believer's resurrection was connected to Christ's, something he had been assuming up to this point. That led him into the answers to the Corinthians' explicit problems with resurrection, namely, the order of events and the nature of the resurrected body. Paul was speaking against a position that denied a future resurrection and implied that hope in Christ was a matter for this life alone. Verses 20-28 were written to refute the denial of a future resurrection and to explain the delay of glorification by describing what was and is taking place behind the scenes. A process of subjection is occurring during which Christ, reigning at the right hand of the Father, is systematically subduing His enemies. All of this is being done according to a unique order (15:23).

The concept of "first fruits" (15:20) was the key to the question of order. Those who were "asleep" had not perished (15:18) but were awaiting their role as "second fruits" of the resurrection. Paul also used the term "first fruits" in 16:15 and Romans 16:5, implying an order of more to follow. Christ was resurrected, but the believers had to wait for their turn. The Corinthians apparently tried to spiritualize their resurrection into a category of this-worldly experience. Paul corrected that error by explaining the chronology and order involved in redemption.

THE CERTAIN LINK WITH RESURRECTION (15:21-22)

Resurrection was as certain as death. As death had entered the world through Adam, resurrection entered through Christ (15:21). As Adam opened the door to death, so Christ opened the door to resurrection life. That was a modal idea ("as" [15:22]). The mode of death in Adam was transmission of his guilt to humanity. The mode of resurrection in Christ was transmission of His life to His redeemed ones. The "all" (15:22) who are made alive in Christ are defined in verse 23 as "those who are Christ's."

THE CERTAIN ORDER OF EXALTATION (15:23-28)

But just as death had taken time to work itself out in history, so also there was a historical order for the outworking of resurrection life. That explained how one could be saved but not yet glorified. Faith in Christ in this life was not all there was (15:19). Each had his own order (15:23): Christ first; then His own at His coming; then the delivery of the kingdom to God (15:23-24).

But why did Paul launch out into a seeming digression about the kingdom's being delivered to God (15:24) and the period leading up to that (15:25-28)? Because he needed to show that the subjection of the last enemy, death, was a process in time. Until it was completed, believers were subject to physical death and had to wait for their personal participation in the resurrection of Christ.

Verse 25 explains the purpose of that period, the putting of all of Christ's enemies into subjection, by alluding to Psalm 110:1: "The LORD says to my Lord: Sit at My right hand, until I make Thine enemies a footstool for Thy feet." The psalm ascribed glory and dominion to the king, with a view to his future total rule over his enemies. First Corinthians 15:25 brings out the significance of the "until" from the psalm. The kingdom would be handed over to the Father (15:24), but only after Christ had subjected all powers.

That psalm was followed in 15:27 by a quotation from Psalm 8.[2] By freely adapting the psalm into his context, Paul drew an important implication for the believers' corporate unity with Christ. He took "until" as the temporal description of Christ's present reign. An equivalence was seen between Christ's reign in 1 Corinthians and the sitting at the right hand of God in Psalm 110:1. Death was the last enemy to be abolished (15:26), not the first. Therefore, the Corinthians would have to live with the fact of death for a while longer.

Psalm 8, quoted in 15:27, spoke of the praiseworthiness of God as Creator and of the inherent dignity that God gave to humanity by placing us over His creation. Though the psalmist spoke of the human race in general, Paul, like the writer to the

---

2. The combination of Psalm 110:1 with Psalm 8:6 is also found in Eph. 1:20, 22; Heb. 1:13; 2:8; and 1 Pet. 3:22.

Hebrews, made that a reference to Christ.[3]

But the order ultimately was not an issue of personal glorification or even of Christ's victory over His enemies. It was all moving to the absolute exaltation of God the Father (15:28). That was a much-needed perspective for those who could not see beyond their own religious experiences.

AN EXAMPLE AND A REBUKE (15:29-34)

In 15:29-34, Paul provided another example to confirm what he had said in 15:20-28, and a rebuke to those who were sinning. To deny the resurrection was to give a false power to death. Dying and raising went together inseparably. To illustrate the manner in which belief in a future resurrection influenced the practical activities of the community, Paul presented two examples in verses 29-32: baptism for the dead and religious persecution. The former related to the state of those gone before, the latter to the ongoing results of faith in Christ.

"Otherwise" (15:29) referred to all the above, especially to the force of 15:20. If there were no resurrection, why be concerned for the dead in any way? The practice of baptism for the dead was not elaborated, leading many interpreters to try to fill in the blanks themselves.[4] The most straightforward sense was that of vicarious baptism for Christians who died without being baptized. Paul, in this context, expressed no opinion concerning the rightness or wrongness of such an action. He simply implied that such concern for the dead would be pointless if there were no resurrection.

Another concern was daily dangers (15:30-32). Why risk death if there were no resurrection, if this life were all there was? The wise conclusion would be that of the proverb taken

3. F. F. Bruce, *1 and 2 Corinthians* (London: Oliphants, 1971), p. 147; F. W. Grosheide, *Commentary on the First Epistle to the Corinthians* (Grand Rapids: Eerdmans, 1953), p. 368.
4. For a balanced survey, see C. K. Barrett, *A Commentary on the First Epistle to the Corinthians* (London: Adam & Charles Black, 1968), pp. 362-64.

from Isaiah 22:13 and quoted in 15:32. Several authors have asserted that Paul did not use the Isaiah passage in its original context[5] but added another sentiment to it. It must be noted, however, that the quotation was not prefaced by an introductory formula and was used in a proverbial manner.

That usage carried the same basic Old Testament sense, a hedonistic attitude in the face of death. Paul did not add a new sentiment to the words of Isaiah, but rather he applied its original sense to another situation. That is a striking example of how Old Testament concepts and phrases become part of the New Testament religious vocabulary.

Exhortation (15:33-34). Some did not know this fact about God. Paul encouraged his readers, by another proverb, to avoid the company of those whose doctrine was infecting the morals of the church (15:33). Just who that group was is seen in 15:34. It was a group with "no knowledge of God"; bad company (15:33) who, no doubt, claimed deep knowledge of God. That the Corinthians fellowshiped with that company was to their shame—a strong blow from the apostle who, in other places, did not want to shame them (4:14).

SPECIFIC QUESTIONS ABOUT THE RESURRECTION (15:35-49)

HOW RAISED? (15:35)

Very possibly the "some" who had no knowledge of God (15:34) were the "some" who asked the question of 15:35. At any rate, that one who asked was, point blank, called a fool (15:36). Those verses return to the question of the delay of glorification due to the divinely ordained order (15:23). Paul's response indicated that the question was asked with a critical, not teachable, spirit. A basic problem with the concept of raising a dead body emerges. But Paul had run across that problem before (see Acts 17:32).

5. E. E. Ellis, *Paul's Use of the Old Testament* (Grand Rapids: 1981), p. 10; F. F. Bruce, *1 and 2 Corinthians*, p. 150.

SEED SOWN (15:36-38)

Paul's answer to his question of 15:35 shows that the problem was with how something dead could come back to life. The analogy of a seed sown provided the point: what was sown was quite different from what sprouts. That analogy provided the basis for the discussion of the main problem, different levels of glory, ultimately with the body "which is to be" (15:37) in view. Therefore, the problem appears to have centered on how mortal flesh could be glorified. But behind any bodily form was the will of God (15:38).

FLESH AND GLORY (15:39-41)

With that foundation, Paul noted the different modes of existence of human beings, beasts, birds, and fish (15:39). Then he extended that to heavenly bodies (15:40). Evidently the Corinthians had a problem realizing that there could be a bodily glory quite different from the one they were presently experiencing. But all through this letter, we have seen them struggling with accepting diversity (leaders [1-4]; liberty [5-6]; idol meats [8-10]; distinctions of glory between man and woman [11]; spiritual gifts [12-14]). The distinctions of this life, however, hinted at distinctions in the life to come. The distinctions of flesh and glory were up to God, as were the distinctions in spiritual gifts. This distinction was between life and resurrection life; there had to be a change in moving from one to the other (see 15:50).

FINAL APPLICATION (15:42-49)

Here Paul combined the sowing metaphor point for point with the truth of resurrection. His four contrasts (15:42-44b) show his view of the nature of the earthly and resurrection bodies.

In 15:44b-49, Paul returned to the Adam and Christ parallel to add support for there being a natural and a spiritual body. His thesis statement was in 15:44b. In 15:20-22, that parallel was used to establish the general fact of death in Adam and life in Christ. Here it became more specific. Christ did not simply bring the possibility for eternal life; He specifically offered life in a form similar to His own glorified body.

To support that assertion, Paul quoted Genesis 2:7. He used the analogy between mankind, as focused in Adam and in Christ, to build his comparison between the resurrection body of Christ and that of resurrected human beings.[6] Therefore, the quotation was not intended to prove 15:44b but to show that what was true regarding Adam was also true regarding Christ. Thus, 15:45b was Paul's commentary on Genesis 2:7. The last half of 15:45 finds no origin in the Old Testament, though some take that passage to be part of the quotation.[7] Contrarily, however, I conclude that it is an explanatory addition.[8]

In 15:46-49, Paul clearly summed up the answer to the two main Corinthian problems concerning death and resurrection. God had imposed a certain order upon the movement from death to resurrection. There was a first and a last to life. The earthly was the first part of the order; resurrection was the last.

ALL MUST CHANGE TO ENTER THE KINGDOM (15:50-57)

THESIS (15:50)

In 15:50-53, Paul dealt with one exception to resurrection: What would happen to those who were still alive at Christ's return? There would be transformation in place of resurrection. True, not all would go through the process of death. But, as an important corrective to the Corinthians' tendency toward premature exaltation, all needed to be changed. Why did he not say "flesh and blood cannot inherit the kingdom of God" at the beginning of his discussion of the resurrection? Because the underlying problem causing the denial of the resurrection

---

6. Crawford Howell Toy, *Quotations in the New Testament* (New York: Scribner's, 1884), p. 179.
7. Hans Conzelmann, *1 Corinthians,* ed. James W. Leitch (Philadelphia: Fortress, 1975), p. 337.
8. See Ellis, *Paul's Use of the Old Testament,* pp. 144-45.

was a view of the present earthly body as already fit to enter the kingdom. Paul expressed his thought two ways (15:50). "Flesh and blood" could not inherit the kingdom. Did anyone think it could? Yes, the Corinthians did, as 4:5-8 indicated. Their problems with resurrection seem to indicate an "I'm already in the kingdom" attitude. But that was not true; even the living would have to be changed at Christ's coming. For the present they were "perishable." The concept of perishable versus imperishable pervades this section (15:50, 52-54). Another way to convey that concept was "mortal" and "immortality" (15:54). Paul continued to elaborate his answer to the question of 15:35. Transformation was another way one moved from the "perishable to the imperishable."

THE NECESSITY OF THE MYSTERY (15:51-57)

The sleep concept arose once again (see 15:6, 18, 20). The "mystery" was the change without sleep (15:51-53). Death was not the requirement for entry into the kingdom—being changed was (15:51). That was reinforced in 15:52-53. The dead would be raised and the living changed. The reason was given again in 15:53. Note the repetition of "must put on" (15:53). Paul was trying to convince his readers who did not think they needed a change.

Isaiah 25:8 and Hosea 13:14 were quoted in 15:54-55. The Isaiah passage spoke of the future blessings that God would bestow upon Israel when all her enemies had been defeated and all reproach had been removed. The Hosea context concerned God's judgments on Ephraim. In His wrath, God would hide compassion from His sight.

There is some controversy among interpreters over the question of whether the Hosea passage was a summons by God for death to come and do its worst to Israel[9] or a defiant challenge for death to try to do its worst.[10] Paul used the Hosea quota-

---

9. James L. Mays, *Hosea* (London: SCM, 1969), p. 181; Barrett, *1 Corinthians*, p. 382; Bruce, *1 and 2 Corinthians*, p. 156.
10. C. F. Keil and F. Delitzsch, *The Minor Prophets*, vol. 1, ed. James Martin (Edinburgh: T. & T. Clark, 1867), p. 159.

tion as a word of salvation; the Christian, in God's victory, defiantly asked death to come and try to do its worst. But, whatever the original intent of the Hosea passage, Paul followed the Greek Old Testament's rendering that viewed the words as a defiant challenge to death. He used the questions as the basis for confident hope of future deliverance. Verse 56 is an interpretation and expansion of 15:55. Death's "sting" was sin. It killed and made flesh perishable. The power behind that death was the law. Paul did not elaborate. A book like Romans shows the fuller thoughts of the apostle concerning sin and law. But for the Corinthians, Paul stressed that the present power of sin (death) and corruption would only end through resurrection or transformation when the Lord returned (15:57; see 15:3: "Christ died for our sins").

CONCLUSION (15:58)

The collapse of belief in a resurrection had caused some to wonder if their toil was "vain." That doubt was weakening the Corinthians' steadfastness and was diminishing the abundance of their work in the Lord. Paul's conclusion reversed their doubts and encouraged renewed vigor in their service for God.

11

WITH A VIEW TO PAUL'S FUTURE ARRIVAL

(16:1-24)

THE COLLECTION (16:1-4)

The final "now concerning" phrase covered the collection for the Christians in Jerusalem. Paul's main concern here was one of order, an order he had also given to the churches of Galatia (16:1). The point of order centered on taking the offering on the first of each week in order to avoid taking a collection when Paul arrived (16:2). The reason for that desire would be given in 2 Corinthians 9:1-5. Titus had already been sent to Corinth to arrange for the offering, and problems were arising (2 Cor. 8:6, 10; 9:2). Paul parenthetically slipped in the remark that the criterion for what someone gave was "as he may prosper" (16:2). A freely given offering from prosperity was Paul's aim. Second Corinthians 8-9 will show the problems that were arising in Corinth to block that spirit of free will.

Another matter on Paul's mind was who would take the offering to Jerusalem. He deferred to the Corinthians' approval for the offering-bearers (16:3) and put his own participation in the delivery into the background (16:4, also in 16:6, "wherever I may go"), a very sacrificial and ministry-oriented position for one whose heart burned with love for his countrymen in Jerusalem. Once again, 2 Corinthians 12:14-18 is a valuable insight into the slander Paul was already facing concerning his relationship to money.

Paul's Itinerary (16:5-9)

The tone of this section suggests that Paul was informing them of a change of itinerary. They expected him to come directly to Corinth. Instead, he would come "after" he went through Macedonia (16:5). This understanding is strengthened by his repeated "for I am going through Macedonia," as if they had missed that the first time.

Paul offered some of the possibilities that his new itinerary could afford (16:6) and then gave the reason for it (16:7). He did not wish to see them in passing but rather wanted to stay for a longer visit. The change in plans created one major problem that Paul addressed in 2 Corinthians:

> I intended at first to come to you, that you might twice receive a blessing; that is, to pass your way into Macedonia, and again from Macedonia to come to you, and by you to be helped on my journey to Judea. Therefore, I was not vacillating when I intended to do this, was I? Or that which I purpose, do I purpose according to the flesh, that with me there should be yes, yes and no, no at the same time? (2 Cor. 1:15-17)

Paul would remain in Ephesus until Pentecost (April) to serve and battle (16:8-9). Acts 19 describes some of Paul's trials in Ephesus, and verses 21-22 express the same thoughts of Paul as this passage in 1 Corinthians.

Timothy and Apollos (16:10-12)

Timothy had been sent as Paul's representative (16:10). Why would Timothy have had cause to be afraid? If the problems in this letter are not reason enough, read 2 Corinthians and see how the situation worsened.

Paul made it clear that he had encouraged Apollos greatly about coming to Corinth (16:12). There was no party-spirit rivalry over Apollos' once again sharing (Acts 19:1) a ministry in Corinth. Also, though Apollos had no desire to come at present, that was due to lack of "opportunity," not to a lack of care for the Corinthians.

CLOSING EXHORTATIONS (16:13-18)

The five commands in 16:13-14 read like terse summaries of this letter. The readers needed to be "alert" for all that would void the cross of Christ. They were not to let problems weaken their "stand" in the faith. They were to embody all that was noble (and Christian) in being "men" and in being "strong." Bonding all those virtues together was "love" (16:14), the truth and behavior that would keep the Corinthians from secular counterfeits of true religion in Christ.

The letter began by discussing the Corinthians' problems with discerning true leadership (chaps. 1-4). Paul ended the letter with an exhortation to obey and appreciate specific church leaders. The exact positions of Stephanas, Fortunatus, and Achaicus were not given, but the basis of their right to honor was. They "devoted themselves for ministry to the saints" (16:15).

GREETINGS FROM AQUILA AND PRISCA AND PAUL (16:19-24)

GREETINGS FROM THOSE IN ASIA (16:19-20)

Paul had spoken often in this letter of the bond of tradition between Corinth and the other churches (7:17; 11:16; 16:1). Here some of those other churches sent their greetings. One church in particular had as its hosts past residents of Corinth, Aquila and Prisca (Acts 18:1-3). Several unnamed "brethren" also sent their regards (16:20).

As a result of all those warm greetings, Paul asked the hearers of the letter to turn to each other and greet themselves with a holy kiss. It is most appropriate to this context to see that kiss as a response to the hearing of the letter rather than a break in thought that commands such action whenever the Corinthians would meet each other for worship. It was a kind of "Give-them-a-hug-for-me" sentiment.

FROM PAUL (16:21-24)

It was common for Paul to end his letters with a brief word in his own handwriting (16:21), the rest of the letter presumably being dictated to and written by a secretary (see Rom. 16:22; Gal. 6:11; Col. 4:18; 2 Thess. 3:17; Philem. 19). Here his final words were a curse, a plea, and a blessing.

The curse was upon anyone who did not love the Lord (16:22). Was that spoken with reference to believer or unbeliever? The entire letter concerned insiders; God, not Paul or any Christian, judges the outsiders (5:13). Therefore, that was spoken to believers. Love for the Lord and love alone was the standard for being included in the sphere of blessing. If love for the Lord was not present, no gift, personality, abilities, or power could qualify a person for fellowship with God.

The plea, "Maranatha" (16:22), was taken from the Aramaic language and meant "O Lord come!" That cry placed the focus on the time when the dark mirror would disappear (13:12) in face-to-face communion with the Lord, and the perishable body would be changed into immortality (15:52).

The closing wish for ever-present grace was the standard end for all of Paul's letters (16:23). But the offer of Paul's own ever-present love in Christ Jesus (16:24) was a unique addition and, in light of the serious and deep problems dealt with in this letter, was the final pastoral expression of Paul's consistent attitude to his beloved in Corinth.

SELECTED BIBLIOGRAPHY

Barrett, C. K. *A Commentary on the First Epistle to the Corinthians*. London: Adam & Charles Black, 1973.

Bruce, F. F. *1 and 2 Corinthians*. London: Oliphants, 1971.

Chadwick, H. " 'All Things to All Men' (I Cor. #IX.22)." *New Testament Studies* 1 (1954-55): 261-75.

Conzelmann, Hans. *1 Corinthians*. Edited by James W. Leitch. Philadelphia: Fortress, 1975.

Dodd, C. H. *According to the Scriptures*. London: Nisbet, 1952.

Doty, William G. *Letters in Primitive Christianity*. Philadelphia: Fortress, 1973.

Ellis, E. E. "A Note on First Corinthians 10:4." *Journal of Biblical Literature* 76 (1957): 53-56.

————. *Paul's Use of the Old Testament*. Grand Rapids: Baker, 1957.

————. *Prophecy and Hermeneutics in Early Christianity*. Grand Rapids: Eerdmans, 1978.

Goldsworthy, Graeme. *Gospel and Kingdom*. Minneapolis: Winston, 1981.

Grosheide, F. W. *Commentary on the First Epistle to the Corinthians*. Grand Rapids: Eerdmans, 1953.

Grudem, Wayne A. "I Corinthians 14:20-25: Prophecy and Tongues as Signs of God's Attitude." *The Westminster Theological Journal* 41 (1979): 381-96.

————. *The Gift of Prophecy in 1 Corinthians*. Washington, D. C.: Univ. Press of America, 1982.

Guthrie, Donald. *New Testament Introduction*. Downers Grove, Ill: InterVarsity, 1970.

Hiebert, D. Edmond. *An Introduction to the New Testament.* Chicago: Moody, 1977.

Horsley, G. H. R. *New Documents Illustrating Early Christianity.* North Ryde, Australia: The Ancient History Documentary Research Centre, Macquarie University, 1981.

Howard, J. K. "Christ Our Passover: A Study of the Passover-Exodus Theme in I Corinthians." *Evangelical Quarterly* 41 (1969): 97-108.

Hughes, Robert B. *Second Corinthians.* Chicago: Moody, 1983.

Hughes, Philip Edgcumbe. *Paul's Second Epistle to the Corinthians.* Grand Rapids: Eerdmans, 1962.

Kubo, Sakae. "I Corinthians VII.16: Optimistic or Pessimistic?" *New Testament Studies* 24: 539-44.

Lane, William L. "Covenant: The Key to Paul's Conflict with Corinth." *Tyndale Bulletin* 33 (1982): 3-29.

Lenski, R. C. H. *Second Epistle to the Corinthians.* Minneapolis: Augsburg, 1937.

Mac Gregor, G. H. C. "Principalities and Powers: The Cosmic Background of Paul's Thought." *New Testament Studies* 1 (1954-55): 17-28.

Orr, William F., and James Arthur Walther. *I Corinthians.* New York: Doubleday, 1976.

Pearson, Birger Albert. *The Pneumatikos-Psychikos Terminology in 1 Corinthians.* Missoula, Mont.: Society for Biblical Literature, 1973.

Plummer, Alfred. *A Critical and Exegetical Commentary on the Second Epistle of St. Paul to the Corinthians.* Edinburgh: T. & T. Clark, 1915.

Sweet, J. P. M. "A Sign for Unbelievers: Paul's Attitude to Glossolalia." *New Testament Studies* 13 (1966-67): 240-57.

Tasker, R. V. G. *The Second Epistle of Paul to the Corinthians.* Grand Rapids: Eerdmans, 1958.

Theissen, Gerd. *The Social Setting of Pauline Christianity.* Edited by John H. Schutz. Philadelphia: Fortress, 1982.

Thisleton, Anthony C. "The Meaning of SARX in I Corinthians 5:5: A Fresh Approach in the Light of Logical and Semantic Factors." *Scottish Journal of Theology* 26 (1973): 204-28.

Moody Press, a ministry of the Moody Bible Institute, is designed for education, evangelization, and edification. If we may assist you in knowing more about Christ and the Christian life, please write us without obligation: Moody Press, c/o MLM, Chicago, Illinois 60610.

549-8926